Focus on Farmers

Focus on Farmers

First published in Great Britain, 2007
by Aune Head Arts in association with Halsgrove

British Library Cataloguing-in-Publication Data
A CIP record for this title is available from the British Library

ISBN 978 1 84114 584 6

HALSGROVE
Halsgrove House
Ryelands Farm Industrial Estate,
Bagley Green, Wellington, Somerset TA21 9PZ
Telephone: 01823 653777
Fax: 01823 665294
Email: sales@halsgrove.com
Web: www.halsgrove.com

AUNE HEAD ARTS
The High Moorland Business Centre
The Old Duchy Hotel
Princetown, Devon PL20 6QF
Telephone: 01822 890539
Email: info@auneheadarts.org.uk
Web: www.auneheadarts.org.uk

Printed in Italy by Grafiche Flamina

Focus on Farmers

Art and Hill Farming

A PROJECT BY AUNE HEAD ARTS WITH BEAFORD ARTS

Contents

Foreword

Ian Mercer

THE WRITERS

To interpret farmers and all their works well to the rest of society, at the beginning of the twenty-first century, is critical to their survival and to the survival of the British countryside – in all its wonderful variety. In that sense alone any attempt at the necessary interpretation is to be commended. I commend this book to you for that, if for no other reason. Its conversations, its poetry, its essays and its images all help the willing to learn more, maybe help the casual to observe more clearly for themselves and help all who pick it up to just begin to understand what makes a farmer tick. 'The rest of society' appears to need the countryside more and more and is, ironically, more remote from the life and work that sustains it than ever before in recorded history. 'The rest of society' includes what I increasingly think of as the political class – perhaps more kindly the political sector, to bring in all the faceless administrators – at least at national level, for its understanding of what makes the countryside work through farming is at rock bottom. This book demonstrates, among much else, the pretty pass to which political ignorance, mince through a bureaucratic

5

machine, has brought a once proud and fundamental industry. For that it is to be commended further.

But farming is not just an industry. *The art and mystery of farming* is the heading of a chapter from A.G. Street's Country Calendar – some will remember those Home Service programmes in the '40s when, among others, he interpreted the countryside to all who would listen at Sunday lunchtimes. Patrick Furse, artist in enamel and son of a mid Devon landowner, created a piece which illustrated his obituary 2005 in *The Guardian,* which reads: "*The care of the earth is the greatest of all the arts*". That's what farmers do, care for the earth... 'and all that grows thereon', we might add, and that is certainly an art. This book is about a variety of artists rubbing shoulders with another varieties of artists, each of both variety a specialist in his or her own part, but the whole is greater than the sum of the parts.

I have generalised, and we must fine down the subject matter of this book. It is about and around a special and specialised set of farmers, hill farmers, or better, farmers in the hills, even farmers in national parks and, in case it escapes your attention, these are south western hills and south western national parks. It may be that that is why I was asked to write this foreword. Before I became a rural bureaucrat I earned my living managing some small parcels of land and teaching about that land and its neighbours and the way it and they worked,

mainly in two magical places, one at sea level on the south Devon coast and one at 1,300 feet in the west Pennines. They were called Slapton Ley and Malham Tarn. In both I jostled with, helped in the work of, and learnt from, farmers. It was the 1960s and farming was still much as it had been for a century or more, despite that century's vicissitudes and hydraulic power. The economic decisions of the late 1940s were only just beginning to modify the patterns of space and time for some farmers, and those few were widely scattered in the South Hams and not at all evident at 1,300 feet.

My first 20 years in the public service was also on a hill – the Dartmoor of this book – and for more than a decade of that I strove with the hard core, the successful, the elite of its strong hill farming community to work out how we might better manage the heartland of the national park because it was common land – their common. That striving resulted in the Dartmoor Commons Act of 1985, a council of commoners to regulate commoning and a duty on the National Park Authority to regulate public enjoyment. In both cases regulation was only as necessary.

During that period the interplay of hill farming and national parkery was made manifest as never before. The intervention and management-by-agreement formulae were invented in an attempt to deal in special places with the land and stock management problems now emerging from those 1940s decisions about subsidy and grant aid. They had led to what the Ministry of Agriculture, Fisheries and Food (MAFF) and farmers called improvement, which in their terms it was but which ecologically and scenically it was not. The new formulae have now spread their tentacles beyond special places and grant aid has evolved into complex Environmentally Sensitive Area (ESA) agreements and 'countryside stewardship' deals, which are in their turn mutating into levels of a new Environmental Stewardship scheme, while subsidy and allowance have, in parallel, coalesced into a Single (Farm) Payment. It all started in the South West, on Dartmoor and Exmoor.

I need to explain my perception of how the farmed hill scenario developed. Hill farming has persisted since that Neolithic hunting genius realised that you did not need to chase animals further and further away from home each day in order to catch the back one, but you might turn them all back, catch them alive and keep them that way, and that was called farming. What we now call hill farming was all farming at first and, like many other cultures, only became confined to the hills as more sophisticated ones developed in easier environments. Its very simplicity as a process and a way of life has given it resilience, and thus a sustained function through all our subsequent social and economic development. That simplicity and closeness to the earth also means the retention of an attractiveness to

the observer, however sophisticated he or she might be. Perhaps the more sophisticated they are the more attractive such a way of life appears.

Two further considerations are necessary. The first is that given that farming in all its forms is essentially the manipulation of natural ecosystems, and that that manipulation is aimed at maximising biological productivity at a point most beneficial to one species – ourselves – then hill farming involves the minimum manipulation and must therefore be the most acceptable to eco-purists and urban intellectual critics. It occupies a place in the human activity spectrum only just beyond hunting and gathering and thus suggests a closer affinity with the so-called natural environment than any other economic game. Secondly, and despite the first consideration, over 5,000 years that ever-so-slight manipulation of the original ecosystem has produced a fairly spectacular change in its primary production layer, namely the vegetation cover. What we now see as the standard and apparently natural cover of the hills – heather and grass moor, western and wet heath – is the product of the farming process. Only the bog remains to remind us that man does not actually have total dominion – in the Biblical jargon. The Wordsworthian quality of the hills, to which he claimed access and called for their national recognition, thus in effect triggering what has now been crystallised in national park designation, has been created by hill farmers. Indeed, the whole satisfaction and pleasure enjoyed by modern man in the hills is a spin-off from a food producing process.

A basic activity of man in his habitat has, quite without thought or 'planning', produced a huge bonus. We have sought to preserve the bonus and the spin-off for some 56 years and still most fail to recognise the logical need to conserve the process that created them, i.e. to keep the hill farmer in place, successful and content.

Equally, just when that bonus is recognised for its real value to society and, like many initial luxuries, is fast becoming a necessity, the fear, in all of two decades now, is no longer of over-sophistication, over-stocking and over-grazing, but of neglect, of total loss, of withdrawal from the farmsteads in the hills of those who know how a man and his stock work together. Without them, the mosaic of plant communities that feed animals, sustain animal biodiversity and stay below knee height – with all the advantages of that – may easily be lost.

So, it is very important that the whole of society, and especially those elected by it to make decisions about its needs and the way its resources are distributed to satisfy those needs, is persuaded to understand what is at stake in the hills now, and what it will take to ensure that the enjoyment of them is unimpaired. This book goes some way to help that understanding.

Long ago I said to a hill farming conference:

"My contention is that fulfilment of the national park purpose demands the conservation of upland management as a human process, a way of life, a production system in order that society derives from the hill maximum yield of protein and the maximum yield of pleasure. They are both mainstays of the life style that lifts us as a species just above the other animals..."

The words embedded in that: 'human process', 'way of life' and 'production system' are as much at stake as the moor and bog, heath and rocks, walls, pounds and linhays to which we have become used, on which we have walked or around which we have worked for the perceivable past and think we wish to work for the foreseeable future. We need it to be a live, and lively, landscape. A landscape where stone walls seem to grow out of the ground but where we know that horny hands helped that growth. If that sounds too romantic, why not? I am with the Greek philosopher who said: "*Had I but two drachmas left, with one I would buy a loaf and with the other a hyacinth.*" Man does not live by bread alone, and all that.

In a word, something more than store cattle and lambs to be finished elsewhere is the product of the most dispersed yet most strongly bound communities that I have known in the hills in which and about which I have worked. Their members are of a broad background; they are a breed I do not want to die out; they are

8

part of my heritage and that of my sons. I want their sons to be there for my grandchildren to learn from, to feed off, perhaps to join (three of them live on a high hill in the north country already). But it is no good expecting – as the conversations in this book make clear – the hill farmer or the community of the hills to live for nothing and without real things to do. Total and complete and satisfying survival with land and stock depends upon a living that earns, that competes with neighbours and rivals, that produces a product valid in its own eyes.

That last point hints at the industrial psychology of the hill farmer and whether it can be maintained intact through however long a period of store-producing instability is forced upon the hills by current imbalances in global trade on the one hand and applied ecological innocence on the other. The whole of British farming is, of course, affected by those imbalances, but the knock-on effect, as curative restriction progresses towards the hills from the eastern England golden triangle, means that the hills are where the effect will last longest, if not forever. Hill farming has been dependent, ever since agricultural specialisation was made possible everywhere else, upon the demand for good stock, to be finished by specialists. In modern terms we have to re-invigorate the brand, re-ignite the demand and thus boost again the 1,000 year-old *raison d'etre* of this splendidly earthy basis of a whole industry which, as it happens, sustains a hill to enjoy, a

hill to challenge and a hill from which to look out. The forebears of those who now sustain that entirely pleasurable set of yields, and who are the meat of this book, were the folk who created the perceived upland landscape in the first place, their 5,000-year legacy is our family silver. It must not be sold... for pounds or euros. Now, read on.

February 2006

Professor Ian Mercer CBE *taught the Dartmoor landscape to students from Slapton Ley throughout the 1960s, was the first chief officer of the Dartmoor National Park Authority, serving it for 17 years from 1973, and was the first Chief Executive of the Countryside Council for Wales. In 1995 he became the first Secretary General of the Association of National Park Authorities, a position he held until his retirement in 2001. He was Chairman of the enquiry into the foot and mouth crisis in Devon in 2001. He was invited to become chairman of the statutory Dartmoor Commoners' Council by its members in 2004.*

Why Focus on Farmers?

Richard Povall & Nancy Sinclair
(Aune Head Arts)

As the work of Aune Head Arts (AHA) is fuelled by a desire to work deeply across all aspects of contemporary Dartmoor, it seemed natural to develop a project centred on its hill farmers. The concept came out of the chaos of the foot and mouth epidemic, which brought human activity on the moor to a halt and saw the destruction of one of the herds on the moor at Dunnabridge. In the late winter and early spring of 2001 there was no stock on the moor and miles of red and white tape closed off commons. Livestock movement and fox hunting were suspended. There were few cars and fewer humans. The moor felt as inhabited as the moon. The events of that spring made it abundantly clear that it was farmers, and farming, which not only maintain the moorland landscape, but enliven it.

Yet farmers are often the last to come to mind when pondering the nature of Dartmoor's landscape. The rolling green fields of the lowland valleys and the windswept grasslands of the high moor conjure up a vision of landscape that seems, above all, natural – a veritable part of 'this green and pleasant land'.

But Dartmoor is a landscape that is *built*. Since the Middle Ages it has been the tinners, the wall builders, the quarrymen, the foresters, the farmers and others[1] who have *built* the contemporary landscape of Dartmoor. The tinners, peat diggers and many of the others were gone by the early part of the twentieth century; the quarrymen left Merrivale when it closed in the 1990s. Those who remain – the foresters, the MoD, the farmers and a handful of others – are responsible for the current evolutionary phase of Dartmoor's landscape. The work of the foresters (who plant, cut and re-plant the conifer plantations) is oddly less notable an influence on a perception of Dartmoor, in that the dense evergreen woods and sections of clear-cut they create is not, in the main, the moor to which visitors flock. The use of much of the north moor by the MoD

(1) *In* Dartmoor Worker, *a collection of articles written by William Crossing for the* Western Morning News (WMN), *were re-published by Peninsula Press in 1992 (an earlier edition from 1966 was long out of print). These articles first appeared in 1903 in the* WMN *under the title "Present Day Life on Dartmoor". In the 1992 edition of* Dartmoor Worker

certainly has an impact upon the landscape, with its observation posts, firing ranges, and detritus, though most of this land is grazed and thus influenced by the farmer. The Dartmoor of today which draws attention and affection is that of open commons, close-grazed turf at the foot of a tor or side of a stream, pony herds, stone wall-lined fields, sheep or cattle tracks weaving through grassland. This is the Dartmoor landscape that farmers create, maintain and change. Their sheep, ponies and cows graze the commons and enclosures. Grass grows, is cut, becomes hay, is baled, turns into black or turquoise pyramids at the sides of fields, disappears and the cycle begins again the next season. From time to time a cow barn, shed or other building appears – or disappears. It is the farmers' activities which most obviously shape the moorland landscape that attracts visitors and tourists; it is the farmers' presence which underpins Dartmoor's economy, culture and vibrancy.

Most visitors assume the land is owned and managed by the Dartmoor National Park Authority (DNPA). In fact, land ownership (and thus management) is exceedingly diverse, and includes the National Trust, the Duchy of Cornwall, the Dartmoor Preservation

Association, South West Water, the Forestry Commission and various private landowners. Of the 235,520 acres within the park's boundaries, only 3,587 are owned by the DNPA. The DNPA does, however ,hold oversight of planning within the park, and is therefore a major contributor to the way the landscape looks and feels.

At AHA we frequently come into contact with local visitors, as well as with national and international ones, in our work and in our private lives on the moor. Many of them spend time here and then leave without understanding the nature of Dartmoor as a living, dynamic landscape – seeing it instead as a kind of theme park preserved by the DNPA for recreational and leisure activities. There might be some surprise to discover that, in addition to the main statutory purposes of all National Parks, to "*conserve and enhance natural beauty, wildlife and cultural heritage*" and to "*promote opportunities for the understanding and enjoyment*" of the special qualities of the national park(s) by the public, each park also has a duty to seek to foster the "*economic and social well-being of local communities*" [2] within them.

As chroniclers of contemporary Dartmoor through the arts, it was important for AHA to develop a project which could reveal the underlying stories about this living, changing

11

the chapter headings reveal much about who was shaping the landscape (and culture) of Dartmoor in 1903, and in the preceding decades and centuries: The Farmer, The Moorman, The Labourer, The Newtake Wall Builder, Swaling, Peat Cutting, The Warrener, The Miner, The Quarryman, The Clay Labourer, etc.

(2) *www.dartmoor-npa.gov.uk/index/aboutus/au-theauthority/ au-ourpurposes.htm*

landscape upon which so many people depend for their livelihood. *Focus on Farmers* gave us an opportunity to show visitors how the 'recreational' landscape they see and enjoy is shaped and has evolved, primarily due to the activities of farmers.

We felt the most productive way of teasing out the stories of the lives of the hill farmers was through a residential project – a departure into unknown territory for AHA. With hindsight, it seems amazing that we had the cheek to ask these farm families to allow us to select two complete strangers (to us and to them) to become a part of their lives and share their homes with them and their children. Perhaps proof of the tenacity which keeps these individuals farming against the odds was shown from the outset in their willingness to open their homes to these strangers, these artists.

Around the time we were preparing to send out the 'call for artists' and making our approaches to the farm families, we had an informal chat with colleagues at Beaford Arts[3] about the project. Director Chris Fogg and Project Manager Clare Fisher were very taken with the concept and asked if Beaford Arts might collaborate with us by co-ordinating a fourth residency on a hill farm on Exmoor.

(3) *Since its founding in 1966 as a northern offshoot of the Dartington Trust, Beaford Arts has delivered high-quality arts activities to the doorsteps of people in northern Devon. Beaford Arts celebrates its fortieth anniversary in 2006 and is England's oldest rural arts centre.*

Without hesitation, we said *"yes"*. Thus *Focus on Farmers* became an investigation into the lives of three hill farms and families on Dartmoor and one on Exmoor.

Intrinsic to the work of AHA is our work with people. AHA is a 'resident' of Dartmoor – we are a member of the community, and as such it is important for us to be, and to be seen to be, a good neighbour. In all our projects we brief artists about the entwined relationships between Dartmoor residents and users (farmers, DNP rangers, ramblers, archaeologists, hoteliers, anglers, riders, foresters, shopkeepers, etc.) and the landscape they inhabit. We do this to establish an understanding of, and respect for, those they may encounter. Our modest library of Dartmoor books is also made available to project artists; it includes books on tinning, walking, archaeology, industrial heritage, Crossing's *Guide to Dartmoor* and his other books, as well as various contemporary periodicals. We told the selected *Focus on Farmers* artists, unequivocally, that we expected them to treat their hosts with respect, as AHA would continue to work on Dartmoor long after the project ended and they had departed.

It was our hope that, by immersing themselves in these farms and lives, the artists would develop work which might inform viewers about the realities of hill farming. When putting out the 'call for artists' we deliberately made the brief for the artists as open as possible, and made no requirement as to artform or type of arts practice. What we were looking for, instead, were artists who were comfortable with an open brief ("*live in residence for a total of 30 days over a 12 month period with a hill farm family and create artworks in response to the experience*") and were happy to work in collaboration with another artist as well as the farm family. To select our pairs of artists we put out two 'calls' – one for established artists living anywhere in the UK, the other for early career artists[4] living in the SW Region. Those selected from these two groups became our 'Lead' and our 'Apprentice' artists. When pairing the artists we deliberately kept those working in similar disciplines apart – thus Hannah Standen, an apprentice sound artist, was paired with lead artist and filmmaker Tony Hill, rather than with lead sound artist Gregg Wagstaff. We wanted to give each of the artists an opportunity to work with someone using a different artform in hopes that it might expand or deepen the practice of both. This strategy worked spectacularly well with Kirsty Waterworth (lead artist, filmmaker) and Beth Hamer (apprentice, working with multi-media and installation), who created all their artworks collaboratively by sharing and melding skills, approaches,

(4) *Central to AHA's work is making opportunities for the SW region's young artists (young in terms of their careers, not necessarily chronologically young). We do this by providing workshops and other training opportunities, as well as by giving them a chance to be involved in residential projects where they can make work and experiment under the guidance of an established artist who acts as a mentor.*

techniques and artforms.

In *Focus on Farmers* we worked hard to ensure that everyone involved in the project – artists and farm families – felt they were central to its success. AHA often uses the ritual of sharing food and wine to bring everyone involved in a project together on a social level; enabling them to share ideas and concerns in a comfortable setting. At the start of the project we hosted a dinner for all the participants – AHA Director Richard Povall cooked dinner for 27, including ten children, and after the meal AHA and Beaford Arts staff washed the dishes. The meal provided an informal opportunity for everyone involved to meet and get to know one another. The farmers were able to eyeball the artists and vice versa. As one of the farmers observed toward the end of the meal, "… *artists aren't so weird after all*…". Another meal was held following a long day of discussions with all the artists as part of a mid-term evaluation – the artists and farmers had such a good time that exhausted AHA staff prayed for the wine to run out so everyone would go home! Throughout the project, whenever anyone had something they wanted to discuss, staff at AHA and Beaford Arts were available at the end of the phone or via email.

At the end of the residential period of the project all the artists came together for a weekend retreat to show their work in progress and to discuss how these disparate artworks could be assembled into a coherent whole for the exhibitions across Devon. At this meeting

Simon Ryder, Exhibition Curator, had an opportunity to meet all the artists and to help begin to determine the shape of the exhibition. This was also the first chance that AHA and Beaford Arts had to see the emerging artworks, and we were thrilled and delighted with what we saw. The FoF artists had truly immersed themselves into life on *their* farms and, through video, sound, photography, weavings, text and sculpture, had created innovative, exciting, challenging and unexpected responses to their experiences.

Over the next few months the artists worked on finalising their artworks, staying in close contact with Simon to ensure that everything would be able to meet his brief from AHA and Beaford Arts, which was to: "... *design an exhibition in which all the artworks can be shown together while maintaining the integrity of each artwork; everything must fit into a Mercedes Sprinter van and be able to be assembled in one day by two people, and be suitable for exhibitions in village halls as well as gallery spaces...*". Simon and the artists came through with shining colours.

Starting from the opening exhibition in the medieval Monastic Barn at Buckland Abbey (a National Trust property), the *Focus on Farmers* artworks toured from April 2004 through September 2005. It was seen in a wide range of venues: in village halls and church halls across North Devon, at National Park Visitor Centres on Dartmoor and Exmoor, at the Exeter Phoenix Arts and Media centre, at the annual conference of the Association of National Park Officers UK, at the Devon County Show and the Chagford Show. During this time over 37,500 people saw the artworks of *Focus on Farmers*. Others took part in a series of 'listening walks' developed by Hannah Standen at Greenwell Farm, and a series of self-guided walks developed by Kirsty Waterworth, Beth Hamer and farmer Phil Coaker at Runnage Farm. The initial goal of using artists to tell the story of contemporary life on hill farms could not have been more successfully met – the individuals who saw the exhibition came from all walks of life, were of all ages and ethnicity and came from Devon, the West Country, the UK and beyond. Much of the work was challenging and even experimental, using artforms unfamiliar to our audience. That it was received so well and with such admiration and enjoyment,[5] bears testament to the grain of humanity that runs through all of the project. The work, in all its forms, is truly an expression not just of a way of life, but of the people and places at the heart of that way of life. To our astonishment, the most controversial element was the set of chairs pulled up to the table with the videos, DVDs and sound recordings. Tessa had been fascinated with the wallpaper of the sitting-room at Warren Farm; a fabric of the same design was found, and Simon had 20 folding chairs covered with it as part of the exhibition.

14

(5) *We know this from comments given to us personally, and from those written in the visitors' book.*

The fabric depicted eighteenth- century style hunting scenes: more than a few visitors commented that we were obviously trying to push a pro-hunting agenda and they decidedly did not approve!

The *Focus on Farmers* project took place over a period of three years, from autumn 2002, when funding applications were submitted to South West Arts (now Arts Council England, SW), the Esmée Fairbairn Foundation and others, to the final exhibition in September 2005. Emotions ranged from sheer terror (Hannah went over the handlebars of one of the quadbikes at *her* farm), to delight (seeing the artists and farmers chatting and joking like old friends at the July 2003 mid-project dinner), to intense pleasure (seeing the artworks in progress at the meeting in November 2003), to a sense of fulfilment (at the opening of the first exhibition at Buckland Abbey, when friends and relatives of the farm families and the artists filled the barn and this wonderful cross-section of people and professions came together as colleagues, friends and equals). There is no way we will ever be able to express adequately our thanks to the Coakers, Coles, Hawkins or Malseeds for making the artists so welcome in their homes and on their farms, or for putting their trust in AHA and Beaford Arts by agreeing to participate in an exploration into the unknown. Nor will we ever be able to explain fully to the artists how proud we are to have been able to show the wonderful work they produced.

The project has ended and we are left with fond memories and a host of new friends.

February 2006

Since 1999, artist-led **Aune Head Arts (AHA)** *has worked on Dartmoor within the context of contemporary rural lives and culture in a collaborative and inclusive manner. We are committed to offering support and professional development opportunities to artists. We are also passionate about engaging with people (residents, visitors, artists and others) in our work across Dartmoor and Devon.*

We believe that everyone is capable of creative expression; that artists can work with a broad spectrum of individuals without compromising artistically or aesthetically; that contemporary artforms can be stimulating, challenging and engaging for all.

15

A Farmers' Conversation

During the mid-term project evaluation at Brimpt's Farm, the farmers came together with AHA to discuss the project. The artists were sent out for a walk in the rain. The following is an edited extract from that conversation.

Nancy Sinclair (AHA): Are there things that we can do to prevent things landing on you at the worst possible times?

Arnold Cole: The trouble is that, on a farm, you don't know when the worst possible times are going to be. It just happened, this morning, one of our sons was away for the day, I was shifting cattle, there was only one son at home who wasn't doing anything very interesting for them [the artists] to follow. So, we felt we were letting you down a little bit by not...

Richard Povall (AHA): I don't think you ever need to feel that, they should be there and just seeing what happens, whatever that might be...

Nancy Sinclair: In terms of having people under your roof, and the meals and everything... is that working ok?

Phil Coaker: With us it works fine, because it's take us as you find us and we're always like that – good days are great, and bad days, you just take it as it is. Sometimes there's dinner at dinner-time and sometimes it's not at dinner-time but we always have it... We've had some great discussions, actually. We've talked about hunting, all sorts of things.

Christine Coaker: It hasn't interfered with us at all, really. They're good because if they can see you are busy they just muck in and help anyway.

Nancy Sinclair: I understand that Hannah had a quad bike accident...

Arnold Cole: Oh yes! They were going along this field looking at the wood, in the middle of this field there's a low ditch, it isn't no deeper than that... then crash... went over the front...

Bridget Cole: Hannah hurt her shoulder...

Arnold Cole: The bike was unscathed that's the main thing (*laughs*).

Richard Povall: Quite a few of the artists have talked about feeling concerned about doing something that you won't agree with, or are concerned about how you think they are going to represent the farm. Feeling like you'd like the farm to be seen in a certain way…

Mike Malseed: I was always on at him [Gregg Wagstaff] about that, because when it started off with Gregg, it seemed to me that he just wanted to do the pretty bits, he wasn't so interested in the dirt. So I kept dragging him out and saying, this is what you should be recording, and he was chasing the butterflies and things *(laughs)*. It is his interpretation, but I was concerned that (and I haven't seen his work yet) people would get totally the wrong impression about what life is like on a farm.

Phil Coaker: I think the important thing to remember is that it is his interpretation.

Mike Malseed: Well I want to make sure that I influence it a bit.

(Everyone laughs.)

Mike Malseed: We finished calving bar two when he came and we hadn't lost a calf up until then, and when we had a cow with a dead calf stuck, he wanted to come and record it and all, and I didn't want him to come and do it. Perhaps I should have done in hindsight, but I thought that the only calving he is going to see is a dead calf and…

Phil Coaker: We started filming one exactly the same, and that soon turned out to be a dead calf and we couldn't shift it. Kirsty stopped and that was that… we would have made about a 36-hour film if she had [filmed it] because we shot the cow the following day.

Mike Malseed: If I was you, I'm sure you think the same, I don't want that on because it will give the wrong impression, because that is a small percentage. Most calving is a good thing, a joyful thing, it is a nice time in the year – I know it is hard work and everything, but it is your harvest isn't it? It's great. But to have one recording of the worst one, to me, I didn't want to do it, really.

Phil Coaker: You know what you are doing, and you know how your farm works and the things that are on it, we know how ours work, and I find that the interesting bit is going to be the interpretation that comes from the artist and what they think. That's what I think will be the interesting bit, what they are portraying. It doesn't make your system any different than it is every other day of the year does it, and the things you do all the time. You've got total perception of that. This is how they perceive it, and that's going to be the interesting bit for us.

Mike Malseed: But if they are coming to it cold, then I think they need steering a little bit *(laughs)*.

Bridget Cole: But, I can't speak for you pair down there, because I don't know you lot *(laughs)*. I think that we wouldn't have got involved if we weren't open-minded people.

Trudy Hawkins: I do think that for those of us on Exmoor, it would have been very nice if Tessa had come earlier and gone through our lambing with us, because it is a big part of your life, and a big part of the farm income at the end of the day.

Richard Povall: That was true for everyone. We meant that to happen, it was just unfortunate.

17

Andrew Hawkins: They have seen a busy time because Tessa was with us when we were doing baling the other day and she was here for the shearing, so they've seen some of the busy time.

Trudy Hawkins: I just think that it would have been very valuable for them to see lambing, what the pressure of lambing is like, the hours. If you are going to paint a picture of farming on Exmoor, or Dartmoor, it is a large part of the farming year. I think it is quite sad that she has missed that bit, but having said that, she's brilliant, she wants to cover everything, she's asked what's an important time to come; she hasn't said, 'I'll be here between here and there and that's when I'll be coming and that's it', but she has said that if something happens at short notice, "*Ring me and I'll come*". Which is great.

Nancy Sinclair: We had hoped that we could get winter into the season, and the grant process took much longer than we had anticipated, choosing the artists and all of that. We had thought the artists could have started as early as February. By finishing in October, they won't get to experience all the fun things that you do in the winter! (*She laughs*). When it is really wet and muddy and cold.

Bridget Cole: They are actually seeing the nicest time of the year.

Trudy Hawkins: Louise has been brilliant. I think perhaps she felt, from my sense of Louise, that she didn't quite know what she was expected to produce at the end of the day.

We've chewed it over, and I think she's now sorted, but she felt a little bit lost at one stage. It wasn't her fault, she wasn't sure what she was expected to do, whereas now... she has been doing some great work with the children too, they've been making felt.

Mike Malseed: He [Gregg] came after lambing and calving and before harvest, so he hit a quiet time. The next time he came, just a couple of weeks later, the weather wasn't right and we weren't doing anything then. He hasn't hit any busy time.

Christine Malseed: He [Gregg] has done a lot with the kids, about the family and on day-to-day living... We went through our list of good points and bad points with the kids, and the farm worker, Jason, said Tania was good looking. We got a lot of positive comments because I took Gregg to a couple of coffee mornings on Saturday mornings and a lot of gossip went on there and a lot of positive feedback! What the kids put on their good points is "*we got pudding every night*"!

Mike Malseed: Bad points. This is Gregg: "*he wakes up too early in the morning (he gets up at half past five to do Tai Chi); he made our room smell of men's perfume; he doesn't eat enough meat; he made us write sound diaries.*"

Trudy Hawkins: They didn't make ours write anything! Our boys are most concerned about Louise. "*She's a veggie, she's never healthy*", they say it all the time. Giles keeps offering her a bit of ham! ... he did go to see some of Louise's weaving and said it was neat. They are not going to last as the sheep are going to rub them all off.

Nancy Sinclair: She has been doing weavings of bits of wool that she's found on the farm with some wool that she brought with her, and then has woven them into fences and various places outside of the farm…

Trudy Hawkins: To see which bits would weather well and which wouldn't…

Nancy Sinclair: She was surprised that most of them are still intact so far.

Mike Malseed: You know we were talking about this censorship thing. I think it is very important, because we haven't heard a finished work yet, but I've heard some snippets, and some of the things they've said in it, they've got wrong, it's just nonsense. Any farmers listening to it… it would discredit everything they've done because they've said something that is utter nonsense. So I think that it is very important not to censor it, but to edit it. That it is run past the farmer first… because sometimes they get completely the wrong end of the stick and you don't realise that they have.

Phil Coaker: We've also had full-blown photos of foot trimming. Now that can be a messy job, purple spraying… Beth and Kirsty have fallen in love with the colours and that's great, that's fine. But at the end of the day, we need to see what is being exhibited, don't we? Because if the wrong people see it in the exhibit afterwards…

Nancy Sinclair: We don't want incorrect views of farming to be put about. Obviously that would negate everything that we are trying to do.

Mike Malseed: You were saying earlier, why do we want to get involved? Well, one of the reasons that we want to get involved is because our farming community always has a problem because most people don't know anything about farming, and it is just one way to try to educate, and better communicate with people. So if you are putting out something that is wrong, it has a counterproductive effect.

Phil Coaker: There will definitely be two different portrayals won't there… there will be our ideal portrayal, and then there will be the artist's interpretation. The two will be very different. Our reason for getting involved was our curiosity as much as anything. And this far in, we are as baffled and still as curious as ever, because we don't know what to expect next!

Richard Povall: Well neither do we, if it's any consolation!

Phil Coaker: Things that I regard as very mundane apparently become very exciting…

Nancy Sinclair: …to sets of eyes that haven't seen it thousands of times…

Phil Coaker: I think my view at the end of the day will be if it doesn't come out as maybe I hope it will, then it won't be us who haven't shown it as it is. If it misses the point that we are hoping is getting through, then it missed the point, but we've done our best. We won't feel that we've been in the wrong place, done the wrong things, we've just done what we always do.

Christine Malseed: I think if all the artists changed farms, they'd come out with something very different... and you empathise with different things in different situations.

Phil Coaker: What would make it very interesting is, at the end of it, you let the host families choose the bits that they feel relate to their life and their work, and the artists choose what they feel, and just see how close it is, or how wide the gap is. There is lots of material, and some will be shelved by the artist because they won't feel it comes up to their mark.

Richard Povall: What might be interesting is to have an exhibition that is put together by you from the material they made...

Trudy Hawkins: It would be interesting to get the artist to pick out, say, 20 bits that they thought really summed it up, because I bet that it wouldn't be... not because they haven't got the point, but because they are looking at it from a really different perspective to us.

Christine Malseed: Not as farmers earning a living, are they? But as artists.

Phil Coaker: Well, we don't *think* so – you might be surprised.

Christine Malseed: Just one final point – you were asking why we were doing it. From our point of view, when we've had bed and breakfast guests in the past, it has been nice to have so-called strangers coming into the house, because it opens up discussion in our household and it makes us think about what we take for granted. It reaffirms what we do. I don't know if you agree with that Michael?

Mike Malseed: Hmm.

(Everyone laughs.)

Christine Malseed: It helps communication having someone else there at the table!

Laughter and conversation as the artists return from their walk.

20

Dartmoor and Exmoor are *the* upland moorlands of the South West peninsula. All those to the west are lower and smaller in area, and while they are all granite masses like their biggest brother, Dartmoor, Exmoor is not granite. Exmoor is formed on the northern limb of a great downfold in the shales, sandstones and grits which underly the bulk of Devon, and one of the most important farming effects of that is that there is very little loose rock lying about on the surface. Dartmoor's slopes, on the other hand, are littered with granite boulders, which may provide walling stone but get in the way and can be a dangerous hazard when hidden in bracken or gorse. Dartmoor overtops Exmoor by some 100 metres and occupies, in national park terms, 100 square miles more (they are 368 and 265 square miles in area respectively). Dartmoor summits collect over 2,500 mm of rain in a year and Exmoor's about 2,000, on the Chains, in the west. Their open country reflects these differences in height, area and rainfall. Dartmoor has two great plateaux of blanket peat, Exmoor some small patches. Western and wet heath surround the Dartmoor plateaux, with grass moor outside that. Heather moorland dominates the northern half of Exmoor, grass moor the southern. That is the context in which the four families of this book live, work and have their being.

Farmed by Bridget & Arnold Cole

Artwork by Tony Hill & Hannah Standen

The 500 acres of Greenwell Farm are worked by Arnold and Bridget Cole, with the aid of sons Neil and Mathew. The Coles live on the edge of Dartmoor's southern plateau at 200m above sea level (OD) but have more in-bye land at 400m, near Princetown. Greenwell, in the parish of Meavy, is referred to in a Pipe Roll as early as 1181 AD. The Coles have common grazing

Farm Film

Tony Hill

Tony Hill filming on location at Greenwell Farm.

Filmmaker Tony Hill and sound artist Hannah Standen were based at Greenwell Farm. Tony's *Farm Film* offers an intimate portrait of life at Greenwell, including an insight into the daily activity of the farm, alongside interviews with members of the Cole family. Tony, who usually works with film, shot on video for this project. Screen grabs from the resulting video can be seen below and on the following four pages.

and 'camera readiness' of video has been useful in the context of the constant, varied and somewhat relentless activities of farming, although this can sometimes be at the expense of more reflective and considered image making. The huge range of activities related to the animal husbandry of sheep and cattle and to grass management, together with the political and family issues, made

"Producing artwork on videotape is a new a different experience for me. The small equipment

the project quite a challenge." Tony Hill, from Final Report, January 2004

rights on a number of commons, of which Wigford Down is a manorial common, and Shaugh Prior 'commons', which, as a unit, form one of the 'Commons of Devon'. They also have rights to graze on 'The Forest', which is now the great central common of Dartmoor and which the Commons of Devon, by definition, abut. The farm has a herd of South Devon and Galloway cows,

A Farming Year

Hannah Standen

Sound artist Hannah Standen created two sound pieces under the title *Farming Greenwell*. Hannah recorded conversations with the Cole family of Greenwell Farm in a variety of locations, the sounds of the farm providing the background to the speech. The following is an extract from *A Farming Year*.

[Sounds of the farmer whistling to his dog to bring in

Arnold: They go to ram in the first of November, they start the first week in March. But they'll all be drenched in dip now and then they'll go into good pasture for a week and then they'll be on a rising plain, where they'll start to jump and play in the field like a bunch of juvenile delinquents going to a party, then wham! In goes the boys [*thumps his hands together*]. Slam bam, thank you ma'am, that's enough, then they're all pregnant.

Bridget: You pick out all the old ewes for selling that aren't breedable again.

[Sheep call to one another and sound of the pen rattling as they push each other inside.]

Neil: You feel this one's udder. Put your hand between her legs… you have to feel both sets of udders. Feel the lump? That means that she won't milk.

the sheep. Thunder of hooves as they run past.]
Bridget: The sheep, they go to ram now. They are in the ramming season.

Tony Hill: Is that mastitis? What's that called, Matt?
Mathew: Mastitis…

as well as pedigree Whiteface Dartmoor sheep (a native local rare breed), Mules and Scotch Blackface. There is also a herd of Dartmoor ponies. Some of the farm's cattle, sheep and ponies run on the commons of Dartmoor. Mathew shows the Whiteface Dartmoor sheep at local shows and at the Devon County Show. For more than 25 years the farmhouse has been used for bed and breakfast; recently a holiday cottage has been added.

Neil: Basically she's got some kind of problem with her udder, basically the canal is blocked. She's not going to milk out of that side, so she's got to go.

Mathew: Can be either mastitis, cysts, abscesses, umm, might have got ripped on something or damaged.

[Inside the farm house.]

Bridget: Well, in October we start feeding cattle to supplement the feed a little bit. The cows and calves in the field will have a bale or two of hay as well as grass, as the grass isn't good enough to keep them going and there is that transitional period where you need that little bit of extra feed before they actually are housed and then they are totally on dry concentrated food, which is hay (dried grass) and silage (pickled grass) and a corn/grain mix.

and they are liable to get calcium or magnesium deficiency, which is what we call grass staggers; but if they are having hay, which is a dry feed cut in the summer, that will help prevent it. It also keeps the grass a little bit longer in the autumn, so that's why we feed cows early, it makes the winter feeding longer, but at least the cows benefit by staying out that bit longer and you don't lose them.

[Outside on the field. Calling the cows, who answer. Sound of cows eating.]

Bridget: And then we start, well, October I suppose, we start feeding fat lambs as well, concentrates in troughs out in the field, before we gradually house the biggest, nearest to fat ones, in the sheep shed, to finish them in there. So again there is a transitional period in lambs.

Arnold: The grass starts to lose its quality in the

Arnold: Because in the autumn, why we start feeding the cows so early when there is still grass, is because you've got big calves pulling the cows,

autumn. It gets shorter, because your October/November ramming, you want all the grass you can to use for your next year's crop, so what we do is that we shut the fattening lambs a little bit tighter and give them trough feed, as it keeps them on a rise and plain as you might say. So that's that. So then we gradually bring them in house. *[Sound of feed into troughs. Sounds of sheep feeding.]*

Bridget: Then the pregnancy is scanned in January or February (depending on which flock it is) to see what lambs they are carrying, and the doubles are kept in the better pastures and are fed a little bit of concentrate so that they have two healthy lambs and have some milk. The singles are expected to live on maintenance diet, because they should be able to have one lamb without too much trouble.

[Dick Brown (Vet) is pregnancy scanning the ewes for single or

> "*The editing process has been long and intense. With so much material, 13 hours of video and 3 hours 30 minutes of audio, selection and structuring has been slow. However, the work has come together well, maintaining the original* Focus on Farmers *perceptions of the landscape and their animals and capturing some of the diversity of activities and issues that make up farming on Dartmoor.*" Tony Hill, from Final Report, January 2004

scanning time because that's when you *(single)* see what the maximum potential of the flock is and see what lamb crop you've got. You can compare it to previous years and have a look at the ewe's body condition *(two)*.

Dick Brown: It helps so you know how to feed them, the doubles need different food to the singles, obviously. And with these *(single)*, if you feed the singles too much and you get a big ram lamb, then they won't come out, not without trouble, and then there's risk to the ewe and risk to the lamb *(single)*. Where it originated in the Scottish hills, the original purpose was to pick up *(single)* the double lambs, because if a ewe on the hills or the moor

double lambs – you can hear him say single or two for the number of lambs inside.]

Dick Brown: There is always a bit of tension at

had a double, the ewe would be in very poor condition *(two)* and she would have only been fed for a single, the lambs would

be in poor condition and she probably wouldn't mother them, and so you'd lose the lambs if not the whole lot *(single)*. That was quite a waste. A terrible waste of life, and economics as well – it's better to have live lambs than dead lambs *(single)*. So it was the Hill Farmers Organisation in Scotland who started it, a chap called Angus Russell *(single)*. It started about 1983 *(single)*, two or three operatives started in '83 and I started in '85 and I've been trying to get it right ever since *(two)*. It's become very much a standard part of people's management now, and it must be *(single)* something like five to ten million ewes scanned a year. Probably five *(single)*.

Bridget: Then they lamb March and April.

[The farmers walk around the barn amongst the pregnant sheep.]

Mathew: These in here, these are all carrying twos. We are going to tail them all out tomorrow or the next day, take the wool around their tail off. See that one there… its full udder. They're not far off dropping. Once you take the wool off their back legs so the lambs can get in at the milk, they will look completely different. You can see, they are really full at the bottom half of their bellies, they are puffing all the time. *[Sound of new lamb calling.]*

Bridget: All the new little lambs, we dip their navels in iodine, and that stops any infection getting in, and that makes them shrivel up and dry up quicker.

Bridget: This little lamb is a bit tiny and perhaps a bit premature, so she might not make it, I don't know. It's got a long cord, and I've got to get it into the pot, which is a bit of an art. Right. See, this little lamb is what we call 'poddle belly', it is a bit rounded, and that's not a good sign. *[To the ewe]* "*There you are mum, there are your two little babies. There you are darling, there.*"

Sometimes the little lambs surprise you. Sometimes they are fitter and quicker and they'll jump up and suck before the bigger ones. That one is a pretty little one, see his brown ears and blacky brown spot on his bum? You always remember lambs like that because they are specially marked. We've had a few come through with little black dots, it's quite nice.

This one here, see the mum is a bit thin, and she's had just one lamb but hasn't quite got enough milk so the lamb's hungry, so I've just got to top him up a bit. The milk might come, but it might be that she's just too thin to rear it. The lamb's healthy enough, it's up there trying to suck, so hopefully… and if she hasn't got enough milk in a day or two, we'll have a mum who's lost a lamb and we'll take it away and foster it to another mum.

Let's see if I've made a big enough hole in the teat and does he want any. *[To the lamb]* "*Are you hungry? Yes, I'm hungry.*" Oh! It's not often that they suck that quickly, so he must be quite hungry. Poor little chap.

[Sound of lamb sucking.]
Must be hungry. *"Aren't you darling?"*
[Ewe makes a noise] Mummy shouting: where's my baby gone?!
Bridget: I'm not convinced she's taken one of those. She's only a young ewe as well. I didn't realise Mathew had put that one in the big pen. I was a bit wary of her when she lambed. She didn't seem interested in either of them when they were born. Anyway, she can stay there for a couple of days and we can keep an eye on her there and top them up. These little things you have to be watching all the time now, and the men aren't very good at that sort of thing *(laughs);* it takes a woman's touch; you can instinctively tell if she's taken both lambs or one

lamb. You'll see them not physically knock the second lamb away, but the second lamb will be lying in the corner on his own where the other one would be cuddled up beside of her, and you think, 'mmm yes', and you are a bit suspicious; so you just watch for a couple of days and you can quickly pick it up. But Arnold and Mathew and Neil, well, they are always in such a hurry...
Arnold: Devon County Show starts spring.
[Sounds of the public address system at the county show.]
Bridget: Then in May you have all the times when you give them injections and drenches. They have all these treatments and injections against diseases that they'll get. Seven-in-one we call it. It is

diptheria and braxy and black leg and pasteurella, etc. The animal equivalent to the children's vaccines, I suppose, is the easiest way to describe it.
Bridget: In July and August we gather the sheep off of the moors – we've got various bits of moors here and at Wigford Down and at Broad Rock and at Sampford, and that's a lovely time of the year, a fun time of the year, where we need extra hands to help to gather because it is such a long way away, especially the Broad Rock flock because they are seven miles away. We need to get the sheep home for shearing and dipping and weaning the lambs and sorting out the old ewes to be sold, so there's lots to be done. But there's also lots of sheep to gather, because everything is there, you've got the old sheep, the young sheep and the baby lambs (but they're not so much like babies that time of the year) and it's a lovely time of the year; the weather is always nice, you can't do it in the rain or the mist or anything, it has to be nice clear weather, and to go onto the moors at that time of the year and experience the heart of Dartmoor is something... I don't know... quite unique, really. You are up there and you can't see anything, any civilisation, which is a really wonderful place, really. I love it, and so does everyone else, there is never any problem, well there is almost arguments on who is going to get to do the gathering, not who's got to do it, so often we all go and I usually take up some sandwiches, a cup of coffee or some

31

drinks and what have you, and we stop and have a picnic on the way home and let the sheep rest – because seven miles is a very, very long way for sheep to travel and we even lose a few sometimes with heat exhaustion or stress and things like that on the way home if we drive them too fast. Mathew always takes the quad bike and the trailer for any who find it too stressful or are a bit weak. They can sit in the little trailer and have a lift home! A tibby bus, as it were *(laughs)!!*

[On the gather]

Bridget: Come on tibbies! They've got a smashing lot of lambs here, actually. There's not one of them who are small or runty. There are one or two limping but other than that they are a really even lot of lambs, which is what you want. Look at those two there, mum and her double, what a lovely pair of lambs.

If you turn them out in good condition and there is plenty of grass on the common, then it's good, but if you turn them out and the mother is in poor condition, they just won't do anything. Dartmoor will keep animals in the condition they go out in, but they won't improve, so they'll just go on looking well and grow more obviously, but they won't fatten.

We started this flock when the boys were… I don't know… seven or eight in the early '80s, and we bought the 100 ewe lambs in Scotland, and we turned them out on the common, up at where we call Broad Rock which is literally a rock in the middle of the moor, it's a boundary stone. Anyway , we put these 100 ewes up there, and then they came in and we only had 80 – we lost 20 in the first year,

and then they lambed and they went back with their lambs, then obviously those lambs went back the next year, and the flock maintained itself at about 100 ewes. Then we started pregnancy scanning the ewes in the late '80s, I should think.

Hannah: How do you do that?

Bridget: Well, just like they do pregnant mums, with an ultrasound on their tummies, not quite so refined as they do with mums in hospitals but same principle.

Neil: Nice ram there. Too much black in his wool, though. If there is too much black in the wool, the wool is worth next to nothing, they can't dye it. They should have nice black and white heads and all this should be white, like that one there, look, it has got a nice black head and all his wool is white.

Hannah: Why is the wool brown at the back?

Neil: That's from rubbing in the peat hags. You know where the peat washes are? They get in there and rub their bum up against it. That one there is a lovely lamb, he's got a pretty head, good black and white legs, a thick body full of meat.

[Sounds of the family having a picnic.]

Bridget: Then they're sheared in May, June.

Arnold: Right through to the middle week of August.

Bridget: Yes, they are sheared between June and August, August the hill flock are sheared.

Arnold: We dip them when they come down from the hill in the summer. It is more for fly striking than it is for scab, but it does the sheep a lot of good to be dipped.

Bridget: Summer dipping is to stop the fly blows

and the maggots on them, which is really horrible. *[Sound of shearing the sheep to pop music on the radio. Sound of dipping.]*

Bridget: Then in the end of July/August, we start to sell a few fat lambs to hopefully get a bit of income coming in again.

Mathew: *[In the field looking over the fat lambs.]* Suffolk Lambs and the dark-headed lambs weigh heavier than the Texel lambs, which are the white randy ones. For some reason they always weigh heavier.

Hannah: Tell me how you feel for fat on them.

Mathew: Basically you feel down their spine, on the shoulder, on the loin and on the tail, to find out how much meat is around that part of the body, and that'll give you an indication of how fat they are. Basically, you feel him, that one's fat, and if he weighs heavy as well, that's it, he's gone, game over. They don't want them too fat. This one was born March/April, so they've been out since then, and they were weaned a fortnight ago. Since they've been weaned, since just being on grass rather than milk and grass, obviously milk is fattening, they've only just started to turn around now.

Bridget: August, the lambs are weaned, taken away from their mum and sorted into the various bunches. Fat lambs are sold and the later lambs are put away on good keep on the other farms. *[Sounds of the men in the fields, moving the sheep and working together.]*

Bridget: Probably August we start to sell in the markets, but it is very little that we sell. We would sell a few breeding ewe lambs, a few old ewes possibly in the markets, but the main reason for using the markets now is to buy and sell rams. That tends to be in September and October, when the rams are bought and sold. Obviously we bred some rams, so they have to be sold, and then we buy in stock rams for breeding purposes, because you've got to have fresh blood into the flock, and the herd for the cattle.

[Busy noisy auction room full of chatter with auctioneer selling livestock in the background.]

Mr. Abel (a farmer): There's enough good farmers on your Dartmoor to breed several, aren't there? And then more people might do it and you might get more in here, and you'd get a proper little set.

Neil: Everybody kisses the bloody arses of the North of England guys, and they are good farmers, you can't take that away from them, but there are enough good farmers down here that we should be able to do the same thing. But if we don't start marketing ourselves better, then… well the Scotch rams down here have got better every year for the last, God knows how long.

Mr. Abel: In the last 10 years there has been a marked improvement.

Neil: A hell of an improvement. With all these ESAs it's only going to get bigger and better stock rather than this small and crappy stuff.

33

Bridget: And then you're back to October/ November when you put the rams in again.

Arnold: Start all over again.

It's the same for the cows, except we don't shear and dip cows, but it is the same. They calf March. April time, we castrate and de-horn all the calves before they go away. They'll make between £550 – £600 pound a piece when they're sold. We've got to wait two years for that, bloody long time Missus!

These go to The Real Meat Company in Somerset. Now because they are a specialised meat company, when these cattle go and be slaughtered, when they go into the butcher's shop, they'll have my name beside of them. When you go into any of their restaurants, they should be able to tell you exactly where the cattle have come from and their history. Look at the steak on that! Cor! Medium rare with a few chips and mushrooms eh? A nice 16 ounce t-bone eh? Cor! Dear dear dear.

The younger cows this year have gone into Down House, 25 of the older stronger cows have stayed home here and have gone over to Chub Tor to be bred pure. The Galloway calves, that calved in November, they've come in with their calves and gone away to Moor until the spring and they'll come in August and be weaned, be PD'd [Pregnancy Diagnosed] and we'll see which ones aren't in calf and which ones are.

Bridget: With the sheep, we lamb them all in the spring, but with the cows we have a spring calving bunch and an autumn calving bunch, so that it is easier to manage, and so that you've also got something to sell all the year round, hopefully. So that we've got a cashflow, really.

Arnold: All about cashflow, missus.

Bridget: Traditionally we used to have most of our income this time of the year, and at Christmas, by God we'd be wealthy! Then you'd be spending that money, a little bit of income would come in the spring, but during the summer we have very little income, really, because everything is growing. You have to manage your money so carefully. With the situation that we're in now, you just can't do it. You can't make ends meet. But by having a cash flow all the time, you know that you need £5,000 a month or whatever the figure may be just to tick over, so if you've got ten fat bullocks in that month to sell, you can visualise that you've got that income coming in and hopefully the income meets the expenditure!

Arnold: If it doesn't, Bridget wants to know the reason why.

Bridget: Yes! That's my job! To keep the finances under control *(laughs)!* Which isn't easy!

Greenwell Barn

**Hannah Standen
& Tony Hill**

The two artists collaborated on the production of a video about an old barn on Greenwell Farm. The following is a transcript of farmer Arnold Cole's reminiscences, recorded by Hannah Standen.

Arnold: **Years ago my father had gone to market, and me and my mother had to milk the cows in the evening** *[calls across from the other side of the barn]* **and my mother was milking a cow just here, and I was milking one next to her. My cow kicked, and I was sitting on a little stool, you'd sit on a stool with a bucket in between your knees milking the cow; my cow kicked, I fell back onto mother's cow, her cow kicked and we both ended up in the gutter here, milk all over, in the shit, and poor old mum was in tears and so was I, and we just sat here and laughed, you know. We weren't hurt, but what a mess, we were all stinking in milk, stinking in cow shit, and we just laughed. I'll always remember that spot.**

But you see my boys won't ever have that, they'll never remember things like that because they are on their quad bikes, they don't have time for one another, really, they don't need to work together as they used to. The family isn't as tightly knit as it used to be years ago because of the speed of life.

My mum and dad had an old converted lorry, they never had a car, they never travelled anywhere, they'd go to Tavistock once a week; that was a big relief, going once a week! I remember when we first had electric and our first television. About 1959/1960 we had a generator, and then when Neil was born in 1971, Bridget

Farmer Cole's words were laid over video images filmed in and around the old barn.

said, "*We can't have a baby here with the generator***", because in the night (when the baby was crying) you'd switch the light on and the generator would start up and it would take a minute or so before the light would come on, well that was no good. So we**

paid £6,000 pound back then to have the mains electric brought in across the fields; that was a lot of money back then. Well then you had a deep freeze, because you couldn't have a deep freeze on the generator because it would keep cutting in and out. I tell the boys some of the things that happened and they laugh 'bloody old fool' you know. This building holds a lot of memories for me, really. Do you know what? Several years ago I hung them bloody bags up in the ceiling and I dunno what's in them *(laughs)!!!* It's a bit of an Aladdin's cave in here really, everything gets put in here and then sometimes you use it. Most of the time you fall over it. *(Hannah laughs).*

See, years ago, I can't remember it, all this building here used to be split up into little buildings. If you look outside here…

bit like a turnip or a swede – and then we used to pulp them up for the cattle. We used to keep all the young cattle in here tied up, and that's what all these stones were for. Along here were the troughs and we used to stand here on the middle piece and you see it slopes away, and that was the old dung pass behind. You see it used to be a hell of a warm building in here. You could come in here in the winter, and you'd have 25/30 cattle in here tied up, and they'd all be looking at you, and you'd go down through and you'd be up there turning the old mangel and you'd be bringing them down, feeding them the turnips. Then over here is the barn where we used to have the hay, and we'd go up there and throw down the bales and then feed them to the cattle. But you see it is so unprofitable now you couldn't do it. It is too time-consuming. Now we've got a house up the top there that we could put 100 cattle in and we can feed them in five minutes. Back then you'd be taking two hours to feed 25. So that's where farming has got to.

Come with me. *[They climb up a series of steps, dogs bark.]*
Hannah: **What's going on?**
Arnold: *(whispering)* They're onto the rats.

Here was the old place where we used to tip all the mangels that we used to grow for the winter feed. Me and my sister, one of our jobs in the autumn was to come over here and pick all the mangels from here, throw them into that corner and build a wall of mangels – a mangel is a

There is a double floor. The reason for that was, in the olden days, they used to bring the sheaves of corn in here, and then they would beat it with sticks. You see the lip here? And there is another lip this side, well when they were beating the corn, that would stop the corn going over and losing it, so it wouldn't go through the floor. You see they had these big doors so that the wind would blow the chaff. They would also bring loose hay and put it over there. This hay is too modern. You're talking about the horse and cart, and sweeps and A-poles.

Hannah: So how long ago did that stop?

Arnold: About 1950. I was born in '47 before Dad had his first baler. He would have had his baler in about '55. It wasn't a square baler like this, it was very soft bales, and then we bought a square baler… you see this is a big invention for us because you can stack so much more.

So that's where farming's got to!

As part of her work reflecting Greenwell Farm, Hannah took a series of black and white photographs that represent activities in the farmyard as well as on the open moor.

A Frame for Farming

Lucy R. Lippard

"We have mixed our labor with the earth, our forces with its forces too deeply to be able to draw back and separate either out. Except that if we mentally draw back, if we go on with the singular abstractions, we are spared the effort of looking, in any active way, at the whole complex of social and natural relationships which is at once our product and our activity."
Raymond Williams

Sculptor Carl Andre once quipped enigmatically that *"all art is agriculture,"* presumably extending another of his statements: *"Art is what we do, culture is what is done to us."* Farmers and artists, in other words, operate on ground level, before culture gets its hands on their activities and their products. At best, artists and farmers also share local knowledge, and can illuminate the places where they work in unique ways. In *Focus on Farmers*, eight artists – from Devon, Somerset, Cornwall, Yorkshire, Bristol, and Fife, Scotland – were called in by Aune Head Arts as 'interpreters' of the hill farms on the Devon moors. (All of our lives are probably foreign to outsiders,

so 'interpretation' is not as bizarre a term for this process as it first seemed to me.) The farm families, from Dartmoor and Exmoor, agreed to open their lives to the artists, who spent at least 30 days with them. This project is a step toward healing the split between agriculture and a post-industrial society, excavating new aesthetics buried in a field often pictured but rarely examined.

Both farming and art have been idealised, and therefore devalued, in our societies. The artists in *Focus on Farmers* are trying to repair bridges, not nostalgically, but pragmatically, by immersing themselves in the practices and places of farming – relatively foreign turf. If the anthropologist's job is to find out 'what's going on here?' the artist's differs only in that 'what does it look (or sound) like?' must be added. Or, from a more personal viewpoint, what is seen/heard and how can that perception be heightened and communicated?

While picturesque farms have obviously been the subjects of paintings for centuries, these artists were challenged to dig far deeper than the 'landscape' of first impressions.

Contemporary art is a framing device for visual or social experience. Trying to catch the texture, as well as the text, of farm life and place, the participants could not be mere tourists, violating privacy to use the lives of others as raw materials for their art. Nor could they be mere observers. To understand this working landscape, they could not settle for the superficial beauty in the eye of the beholder, who is often just passing through, unaware of the chill of damp air, the squoosh of wellies in the mud, the strength of the wind, the contrast between compact fields and the open moor, or the sore muscles during a long day's work that will be repeated daily for a lifetime. Somehow an exchange had to take place – a synthesis of two very different experiences into a product that could be understood by everyone.

The place is the mediating force. It may take longer to be truly familiar with a mute place than with talking people, but in both cases individual experience leads to a clearer sense of communal experience. The real story is told by traces on the land of geological, biological, and anthropological use – the vast spaces in sight and the detail found underfoot. These are of great interest to visual artists, not merely as forms and colours constantly changing when light and shadow sweep over them, and not only as raw materials, but also because of what they have to say about who we are, what cultures and ecosystems have lived and merged and disappeared in this place.

Most landscapes are designed by culture, mostly at the hands of anonymous amateurs who privilege function over form. Later, hired professionals may try to make sense of what's there and capitalise on it with their own individual talents. The very term 'cultural landscape' is a way of thinking about art and landscape issues that was partially invented by J.B. Jackson, a peripatetic scholar and seminal cultural geographer, who defined it as "*a concrete three-dimensional, shared reality*" – a collaboration between people and nature rather than an idealised picture or view of what's out there beyond our own centre.

Collaboration is the core of this enterprise, and the journey toward that shared reality can be a hard one. Art is popularly perceived as hoity-toity and above it all, a hobby or leisure activity rather than serious work – this despite the fact that artists themselves often identify far more with workers than with the bourgeoisie who form their clientele. There are inevitable class divisions between some of the artists and some of the farmers, at least until a bond is created on the basis of the land and the work. Hill farming is a subculture of British farming culture, which is in turn very different from that elsewhere in the world, the Americas included.

Kirsty Waterworth and Beth Hamer – both from Devon – worked as a fully collaborative team, and a busy one at that. They made a guided tour book around Runnage Farm, led a walk/workshop for school groups with farmers Christine and Phil Coaker, made a neon and granite installation based on the farm's Defra number, a video installation projected onto screens made of live grass, and a standing 'chandelier' made from recycled tractor parts.

At the other extreme, Tessa Bunney and Louise Cottey worked independently with the Hawkins family at Warren Farm. Cottey, a textile artist, wove various found materials onto fences and elsewhere in an interesting play on raw materials and production. Bunney made striking photographs in which animals and places take on new life – stunning 'still lifes' of a blacksmith at work, the head of a curly-horned ram with closed eyes, a warm working kitchen seen through a window at night, the heads of serious children at a fox hunt as a marginal frieze against a huge blue sky. Having worked as a photographer with community issues in Yorkshire, including a series of *"environmental portraits of farmers and small food producers and the lives of hill farmers on the North York Moors"*, Bunney's truncated images, odd angles and expanses of sky transform daily activities into sheer beauty that must surprise even those whose lives are pictured.

Hannah Standen's CD *Farming Greenwell: sounds of a contemporary hill farm*, Tony Hill's video *Farm Film*, and their collaborative video *Greenwell Barn* offer fragmentary narratives that bring us closer to familiarity, becoming a composite portrait from several angles: vociferous animals, running water, clanking tools and old machinery, a chorus of hungry baby lambs, and, above all, the voices of the farmers – Arnold and Bridget Cole and their sons Neil and Mathew – explaining the fascinating mechanics of hill farming. From the summer dearth of income when 'everything's growing' to the hopeful marketing time, from joyful family picnics while gathering sheep on the moor to the dwindling local markets with their social networking and reinforcements being replaced by the sheep just 'going away in a lorry' to the meat companies. Yet, as Bridget Cole insists, *"It's never money in the bank. We're only lifetime tenants on that land and then the next generation comes along. It really is a labour of love."* And it's a matter of pride: *"A good farmer will want to give more to his son than his father gave him... leaving the land in better condition than when you got it from your father."*

Yet life on farms is changing drastically. Administration is taking priority over animals. Since the Second World War farms have gotten larger and the workforce has gotten smaller. Hill's video sometimes speeds up to reflect the pressures; sheep stream by, their heads bobbing, men muck out the cows' stalls and frantically shear one animal after another. Farmers (or 'countryside technicians') are resigned to the fact that farming is no longer valued as it once was. *"People see it as a way of life and not a business,"* but, *"first and foremost someone has to make a living off the land."* Hobby farms bring down the prices. (A 'fat cow' brought more money 20 years ago than today.) The more the moorland commons is 'diversified,' opened up to recreation and tourism, the more the farmers are dependent on subsidies and the more the government controls the way they farm. In all the efforts to keep the moor 'the way it is', outsiders fail to realise that it is that way because of the sheep and the farmers, the way it has been managed for so long. "*They'd rather listen to an ecologist than listen to one of us who's been here for centuries… You can't start and stop a farm,*" says Arnold Cole. "*It's like a big snowball, actually.*"

Gregg Wagstaff and Tania van Schalkwyk, on Frenchbeer Farm, collaborated with Mike and Christine Malseed and their four children to create an encyclopaedic sound-and-image portrait of this extraordinarily articulate 'ordinary family' and their work. (For the exhibition, they also created a chaise longue with sheep's fleece and provided a pair of ram's horn headphones to hear van Schalkwyk's Frenchbeer inspired poems.) From casually drawn 'sound maps' marking such banally diverting moments as a dog yawning and alarm clock sounding off, to children's 'sound diaries' (in one of which Richard Malseed howls like a dog, mimics a lamb on a spit made from a bike chain, the splash and run of a river, the pitter patter of rain on the slate roof), to audiotapes of a birthday party, swimming antics, a children's race… and hours of oddly riveting and detailed conversations about seed, feed, poultry, cattle, sheep in sickness and in health.

The Malseeds have been on their farm for only 18 years, but Mike is eloquent about his role in maintaining "*my bit*" of a manmade landscape thousands of years old, "*making sure it's not sold off*" for someone's holiday house or second home. He contends that a farmer needs three things: a dog, a 'quad bike' (a motorised vehicle that has taken the place of horses, though he rode a horse before he could afford one) and a crook. "*The dog would be the last to go.*" Christine works as a business advisor to other farmers in the region, as well as keeping the home and the books, so her view is invaluably both wide and narrow. Her account of the devastation wreaked by the foot and mouth disease crisis testifies to its all encompassing effects, from halting local social life to severing bloodlines that went back generations. The Malseeds, like their counterparts at other farms, make clear that it is not financially viable to maintain the landscape as a farm. "*We farm because that's what we're good at, but we're turning into land managers.*" (or 'habitat conservationists'). And they bemoan the loss and probable downfall of the Dartmoor ponies, which now have to have their own expensive 'passports' (as do cattle) if they are off the moor, as they sadly send three of their own off to the abattoir. Death is very much part of all these stories.

Photography (which itself has been called a metaphor for death) is the chosen medium for several of the *Focus on Farmers* projects. It can produce a seductive but alienated image or it can be a tool with which to understand place. I like to think of a photograph as a *field*

41

rather than an *artefact*, suggesting sequence, layers and periphery. Even when the number of images is limited, the implications must go beyond the frame, inspired by what has been chosen for within the frame. We look at documentary photographs as pieces of a puzzle that will never be complete except in our own imaginations. Yet old photographs, especially those showing people who will be recognised by locals, can help us communicate about the lay of the land. Places look different to those who have experienced them differently. (As a local land-based man in Roswell, New Mexico told an artist working there, "*Most educated people say, where is it written? Our people say, where is it lived?*")

If topographies change at a glacial rate, the cultural landscape is constantly transforming and so are we, its inhabitants, its transformers. A cultural map may be all centre and no margins, also a definition of the truly local, where each centre within a centre is connected by paths to other centres. Place names offer clues (Dartmoor's monikers roll across the tongue like the moorland itself) and trigger memories. Few of these works could have been executed without a good deal of walking, which is the prime means by which to experience landscape and place. It is no accident that walking as an artform was pioneered by an Englishman, Richard Long. The variety of open trails through the countryside in the UK is unknown in the US, especially in the west, where trespassers are shot or arrested. (We are only now trying to set up a trail system in the rural New Mexico valley where I live.) Even these days, walking remains crucial to working the land, especially on the relatively small scale on which agriculture takes place in England. And walking is the best entrance for outsiders into a sense of place.

I once lived on an old stone farm near Halwell, Devon. It was my first year-round experience of rural living and it changed me and my work, just as the stone rows and circles and dolmens on Dartmoor altered the way I saw the potential for a public art, and Public Works from nearby Dartington Hall expanded my notions of community theatre. When I returned to New York I could visualise, step by step, the long-ranging walks I took every day with a treasured border collie: the spring of turf underfoot, each topographic turn, and the courteous farmers I ran into in my wanderings. My ancestry is primarily British and the connections overwhelmed me.[1]

Today I live in an arid high-desert ranchland in New Mexico that was once a farm village and is now a bedroom community. It couldn't be less like the English countryside. Still, the Devon lessons in studying place remain my base. I may know this land better than I did 'my' patch of Devon, but Ashwell Farm is as real to me almost 30 years later as my present home is. Yet when I returned there a few years ago, each of the old stone barns had been made into a fancy second home. New houses

(1) *See Bunce M. (1994)* The Countryside Ideal: Anglo-American Images of Landscape, *London and New York: Routledge.*

cluttered the valley. A tennis court had replaced the slurry pit. Those fields are now better walked in memory alone.

Rural gentrification doesn't get a lot of attention in the US, but having been one of its agents, and as a neighbour to threatened ranchlands lying in the path of development, I often think about it. Living in the North American west for the last 20 years or so, I've become increasingly conscious of 'land' as a distinct spatial and spiritual element, as well as the raw material for habitation and agriculture. As soon as working farm landscapes are in danger, many more of us discover how attached we are to them, how rooted they are in our communal memories. Even as the presence of place, and its often agricultural past, is diminished and lost, it continues as an absence to define culture and identity for us restless, multicentered and multitraditional people.

History and heritage seem inseparable from the English landscape, which, in much of the Western world, has come to epitomise 'countryside', rooted in our topographic memories. It is the 'landscape' we conjure up when thinking of pastoral painting and 'farming'. Yet all farmland today is contested land. Continuity vies with disruption as flattened fields and stark metal farm buildings stick out like sore thumbs in the English landscape, interrupting those comforting, visually organic compounds of old buildings nestled amidst rolling hills that still survive in Devon. For 'agribusiness', on the other hand, we picture the American Midwest. Robert Riley, writing from Illinois, distinguishes between the *"old rural landscape... a place where people worked on the land, earned their living on the land, and lived on that land"* and *"the new rural landscape... a residence and occasional workplace for people whose livelihood depends not at all upon the land per se."*[2] Rural places are no longer *"a productive system"* but a *"locational amenity"*, no longer based in a *"clear visual order"*, but subject to *"buckshot urbanization"*, as Richard Louv has put it.[3] Today there are even annual conferences on marketing 'agri-tourism'. Landscape architect Carla Corbin has unearthed a kind of virtual agri-tourism, fascinating testimony to the deep attachment even longtime urbanites and suburbanites hold for the earth in our pasts: the CornCam website, which allows the agriculturally alienated city dweller to watch corn grow at 15-minute intervals. Its international popularity was huge and unexpected. CornCam could easily be mistaken for a postmodern, minimal, vaguely ecological artwork, but it was produced by the magazine *Iowa Farmer Today*, beginning as *"something of a joke.... A digital version of the custom among farmers to drive around Sunday afternoons to check the progress of each others' fields"*. But, as Corbin points out, this kind of documentation

43

(2) *Riley R. (1993) "Thoughts on the New Rural Landscape"*, Places, *v.8 no.4, 85.*
(3) *Louv R. (1983)* America II, *Boston: Houghton Mifflin, quoted in Ibid, 89.*

is not the usual country kitsch. The footage is not picturesque or pictorially appealing. It is *"visually boring, more like a factory, which is what it is"*.[4] Yet however removed, it provides access to nature and, through nature, for those no longer even familiar with nature, access to the Jeffersonian national identity from which we Americans have been separated by time and space.

Right now our cultural use of nature is too often to make it stand for what we are unwilling to stand up for. Although few colleges (Dartington College of Arts among them) are teaching this kind of work, which would speed up the process considerably, an increasing number of artists are taking things into their own hands and independently qualifying themselves to develop a truly place-specific public art. As an embattled American, working with private land trusts and watershed protection under the rule of a national administration that dismisses and destroys the environment, I envy British organisations like Aune Head Arts and Beaford Arts. The renewed interest in rural arts taking place in the UK has not been replicated in the US, but there are a number of artists who have independently begun to work with farmers, among them Sabra Moore, who runs the Farmer's Market in Española, New Mexico and has made art from her growers' stories, transferred onto long muslin banners for a local 'Farm Show'. Nick Tobier taught an art class at the University of Michigan called 'Food From Farming to Feast' that included an oral history project with local farmers. Sam Easterson, working with the Center for Land Use Interpretation, has done a witty turnaround on documentary photography with a show called *On the Farm: Live Stock Footage by Livestock*, in which wireless video cameras were installed temporarily on the heads and necks of sheep and cattle, showing what they look at, how they move through space and how they relate to each other. Linda Gammell and Sandra Menafee Taylor, who 'grew up rural' in Minnesota, have worked with various collaborators on artists' books and installations on farm lives. They quote Wendell Berry: *"The good farmer, like the good artist, performs within a pattern; he must do one thing while remembering many others."*[5]

Farm policy in the US is every bit as confused as it appears to be in Britain. The fragility of the family farming sector and of threatened agricultural land has finally become apparent to conservationists realising that wilderness is not the only open space, that place consists of both land and people. Yet, on the whole, artists seem reluctant to become involved in real-world issues such as economics, or land

44

(4) *Corbin C. (Spring-Summer 2002) "American National History and the New Landscape of Agriculture: Scale, Power, and Abundance",* Journal of American & Comparative Cultures, *65-80.*

(5) *Berry W. (1989) quoted in Blatti J., Gammell L. and Menafee Taylor S., "SE ¼ Section 6, Township N, Range 21 W of the 5th Principle Meridian 160 Acres: Landscape of Hope and Despair" (artist's book) Minneapolis*

use and management – the invisible subtexts to all farm/art projects on both sides of the Atlantic. Geographer George Henderson writes: "*Landscape, like race, gender, or capital, has a conceptual life, a life of usage, that is ripe for analysis.*" (The word ripe works well here, ready for picking.)

Place-specific artists (not the same as 'site specific', which lends itself to a more abstract placement of art in 'the landscape') need to be familiar not only with the people but with the bedrock, the infrastructure of the place they are perusing. There is some question about whether documenting change is enough; certainly just reflecting it is not. What happens when the artists leave? Has anything changed for those photographed and recorded? Without a sense of place, community-based environmental activism is just a generalisation. Forget the 'Lucky-you-I've-come-to-make-art-for-you' syndrome. Communities educate artists. The *Focus on Farmers* participants are showing the way for documentary artists who don't just hit and run but stay and live, exploring the relationships between people and place that makes family farming what it is. And in turn the artists have made the farmers more aware of the sights and sounds that surround them.

This *exchange* is crucial to the development of more art activism, not just reactive NIMBYism – what we don't want to happen in our backyards – but a proactive stance about what we *do want* to happen there. Even a moving population can take responsibility for

wherever we find ourselves at the moment. We too can study the ways in which cultural regionalism and ecological bioregions overlap and how artists might illuminate and expand this experience with the communities in which they work. Society produces nature, but artists should be able to produce new angles on seeing nature and place that will, in turn, affect the way we treat the natural. Perhaps art about agriculture or nature itself will not be fully effective until it goes underground, until it is integrated into and almost disappears into local culture and nature itself. In any case, Britain, with its respect for the past and rural traditions as well as a thriving avant-garde, is well positioned to support such art, and *Focus on Farmers* is a major event in this continuum.

This essay repeats and expands on themes first explored in my book The Lure of the Local: Senses of Place in a Multicentered Society *(New York: The New Press, 1997).*

Lucy R. Lippard, *writer and activist, is one of America's most influential art writers. She has published 20 books on art and cultural criticism, including* The Lure of the Local, *an exploration of our multiple senses of place, and* On the Beaten Track: Tourism, Art and Place, *as well as* The Pink Glass Swan, *essays on feminist art. She is the founding editor of El Puente de Galisteo, a monthly newsletter in her rural New Mexico town, and once lived for a year on Ashwell Farm, near Totnes.*

Devon Farming

Anthony Gibson

"I have been in all of the counties of England", declared Oliver Cromwell", *and I think the husbandry of Devonshire the best."* And however anxious the Lord Protector may have been to ingratiate himself with the locals when he made that remark, I have no doubt that there was more than a grain of truth in it.

Devon has always been pre-eminently a farming county. Its characteristic landscape of small fields, big hedgebanks and narrow, winding lanes is as it is because of the way the land has been farmed; not just recently, but going back for over 1,000 years. Even Devon's towns and villages bear the imprint of agriculture, for many of the county's most magnificent churches and handsome vernacular buildings were built on the proceeds of the medieval woollen industry. For all the glories of its coastline and exploits of its sailors and traders, it has been farming that has given Devon its identity. When people think of Devon, they think of red soil, clotted cream and cider.

And even in the first decade of the twenty-first century, farming is still hugely important to the county. It contributes around 2.5% of the county's gross domestic product and supports 6,000 jobs directly, and another 10,000 in the businesses that provide farming's inputs or process its outputs. Even after all of the structural change of the last half century, there are still at least 6,000 genuine farms in Devon – substantially more than in any other county – producing milk, beef, lamb, corn, oilseeds, pigs, poultry and an ever-growing range of fruit and vegetables, all worth over £250 million at the farmgate.

Farming matters in Devon, and it matters *to* Devon as well, perhaps to a greater extent than in any other county in England. From which it follows that if farming is facing the biggest changes in more than half a century – which, thanks to a radical reform of its policy framework, it is – then so too is Devon, and especially rural Devon.

However, to understand what the nature of those changes may be, and their possible wider impacts, it is necessary first to understand what makes farming in Devon tick, and to understand that, we need first to turn to a little history.

Even as early as the mid-seventeenth century, when Cromwell was speaking, Devon was a county of yeoman farmers, blessed with the independence and security to make the very most of the inherent fertility of their land. There were open field systems of farming in the county – Braunton Great Field being the most notable example – but they were very much the exception. It would appear that Devon farmers were no better at co-operating in medieval times than they are today!

By the 1600s, most of the land was farmed either by freeholders or under secure, long-term tenancies. The custom in Devonshire was to let land for a period of 'three lives,' or 99 years, whichever was the shorter. In practice, as both of the successors named by the initial tenant had to be living, the three lives always ran out before the 99 years had elapsed. But the terms of the lease allowed other names to take the places of those that fell by the wayside, so that the leases could last for centuries. As W.G. Hoskins concluded in his *Devon*, "*the standard of Devonshire farming owed much to the terms on which the land was held*".

If one was looking for an example of that, one need look no further than the Quartlys of Molland, on Exmoor. They were tenant farmers, but the security that they enjoyed provided the strongest possible foundation on which they could build the project that made their name immortal – the perfection of the Devon breed of cattle. In their day – and this was the heyday of livestock breeding, when prize specimens would tour the country to be exhibited in front of huge crowds – the Quartlys were as famous in their way as was Thomas Bakewell with his Leicester sheep or the Colling brothers with their Shorthorns.

But this was the high-water mark for Devon farming. A system of land tenure that had been an asset for so many years became, in the end, a handicap. Ingoing tenants were required to pay higher and higher premiums for taking on their leases. All too often, this left them with heavy borrowings and insufficient working capital. It led to land being exploited ruthlessly to meet the financial imperatives. The old adage of "*live as if you might die tomorrow, but farm as you would live forever*" went out of the window, and with it went Devon's reputation for farming excellence.

Whilst the county shared in the unmatched prosperity generated by the Napoleonic Wars (in 1805 the price of wheat reached the equivalent of £1,450/tonne, as against £85 today) investment for the future seems to have been the exception rather than the rule, and by the late-nineteenth century farming was in no state to cope with the combined impact of a series of disastrous harvests at home and a flood of cheap corn from a USA no longer riven by civil war. And in the meantime, of course, the repeal of the Corn Laws in 1846 had stripped away the protection that British farmers had enjoyed against being undercut by cheap imports since the fourteenth century. The chickens that the anti-free trade league had warned against so vociferously whilst the Act was going through Parliament had come home to roost with a vengeance.

The pattern had been set for a depression that lasted for almost 70 years – barring a brief resurgence during the First World War, when the country needed every ounce of food it could produce. By 1939, Britain's farmers were producing only enough food for a third of a population of 48 million people. In Devon, the arable acreage had fallen by almost a quarter of a million acres from its peak in 1872, with over a million acres down to permanent grass and rough grazing. Thanks not least to the creation of the Milk Marketing Board in the early 1930s, pastoral Devon was not hit as hard as arable East Anglia, but it was still an era when grinding rural poverty was the rule rather than the exception.

Not that the government was greatly concerned. A very conscious decision had been taken, almost a century previously, to import food from wherever in the world it could be obtained most cheaply (which was usually the Empire), so keeping food prices down, wages in check and ensuring the competitiveness of the manufacturing industry that was the mainstay of the British economy. Such was the cheap food policy; and it was deeply engrained.

Through the good times and bad, plenty and paucity, war and peace, the yeomen farmers of Devon ploughed their accustomed furrows. Families rolled on from generation to generation, seemingly impervious to what was happening in the wider world. The conservatism and thrift that seems to have inhibited the adoption of new techniques in the wake of the agricultural revolution of the late-eighteenth century, served the rural community well when it came to surviving the long depression 100 years later.

In fact, in many ways this was an era of opportunity. Land was cheap and rents were low. A good farmer with an appetite for hard work could get on. I think immediately of Dick Darke, one of the greatest Devonian stock breeders of the twentieth century, who not only created a hugely successful family farming business at South Huish through the 1930s, but had a lot of fun doing it as well.

I stress the resilience of the Devon farming community, because it is a quality that has been much in demand in the recent past, and which, I suspect, will be tested to still greater extremes over the years ahead. Take the 2001 outbreak of foot and mouth, for example. If anything was likely to produce an exodus from the land, it was that. It came, after salmonella, BSE, swine fever and bovine tuberculosis, as the last and most traumatic epidemic in two decades of pestilence. It followed a year in which farm incomes reached their lowest ebb in modern times, and it coincided with the re-election with a thumping majority of a Labour Government widely perceived as having neither sympathy for nor understanding of the countryside, whose only substantive commitment in terms of rural policy was to abolish hunting! And on top of all that, the weather was filthy.

Morale among the farming community in Devon can never have been lower than it was in the spring of 2001. If ever there was a time to quit farming, then this was it, especially if you had just witnessed the slaughter of your life's work before your very eyes, and been in receipt of a compensation cheque that represented probably more money than you could expect to earn from 20 years more slogging your guts out milking cows.

So how many of those foot and mouth victims took advantage of what was a heaven sent opportunity to make a graceful exit? Hardly any of them. During the autumn of 2005 I sent a one-page questionnaire to the 174 Devon farms that had actually had the disease, asking what had happened to their farming operations in the interim. Of the 103 who replied, only two had given up farming and were now working in another business or industry. Of the remainder, 15 had let their land and taken semi-retirement, but by far the biggest proportions had either re-stocked and carried on much as before (21%) or re-stocked and used their compensation to expand (24%).

It therefore comes as no surprise at all that a survey carried out in 2005 by the University of Exeter Centre for Rural Research[1] found that, despite the threats and opportunities offered by the advent of the Department for Environment, Food and Rural Affairs (Defra's) de-coupled 'single farm payments', some 60% of a large sample of farmers expected to be still in charge of their farming businesses in five years' time, with another 20% planning to hand over to their successors within that time frame. Of the

remainder, only about a third (6% of the total) intended to quit farming altogether, with a similar proportion planning to keep their land but allow someone else to farm it.

Now, the possibility of up to 12% of Devon farming businesses shutting up shop over the next five years is not a prospect to be taken lightly. But then, nor does it amount to farmageddon. Farmers in Devon appear to be similarly sanguine as to the nature of their businesses. Despite all the talk of the advent of the single farm payment representing a 'revolution' in agricultural policy that would usher in a 'sea-change' in farming practice, by far the largest proportion of farmers in the Exeter survey – 45% – admit to being engaged in what might be described as 'traditional re-structuring': cutting costs, buying a bit of extra land, changing enterprises and so on. The sort of changes, in other words, that farmers have been making to their businesses since farming began.

At this point, it is probably worth providing a brief explanation of how single payments will work, what they will mean for farmers and why people like me are talking about revolutions and sea-changes, triumph or disaster. Farm support policy has gradually evolved since it was reintroduced in this country some 65 years ago. In the Second World War and afterwards, its avowed aim was to provide stable, profitable, 'guaranteed' prices for farmers that would enable them to step up production and reduce the nation's dangerously heavy (as it certainly

49

(1) *Lobley M., Potter C. and Butler A., with Whitehead I. and Millard N. (2005)* The Wider Social Impacts of Changes in the Structure of Agricultural Businesses Report to Defra *Centre for Rural Research, University of Exeter*

was in 1939) reliance on imported food. The policy was a resounding success. By 1973, when we joined the European Economic Community and began the process of transition to the Common Agricultural Policy (CAP), the volume of food produced in Britain had well-nigh doubled, as compared with 1939.

By contrast, the principal aim of the CAP was to raise rural standards of living, and it attempted to achieve this through a managed market system that guaranteed farmers a profitable price for their products. That inevitably led to surpluses, which then had to be taken off the market and either put into intervention store or dumped on the world market with the aid of huge export subsidies. By the early 1980s it had become clear that the policy was not sustainable, in any sense.

So it was progressively reformed, with quotas and set-aside being used to limit output, and prices being cut, with farmers being compensated through headage payments on livestock and area payments on arable crops.

It was on these payments that the 2004 CAP reforms were focused. In the jargon of the EU, they were to be 'de-coupled'. Stripped down to its essentials, what that meant was that, from 2005 onwards, the farmers would be paid their headage and area payments without having to keep the animals or grow the crops. Member states were given the option of taking the process slowly, by either delaying the changes or implementing them in stages. In the UK, the government decided to go the whole hog at the earliest opportunity. Not only that, but in England, a payment based on the farmer's historic receipts from the production subsidy system would gradually be replaced by a flat rate payment, the single farm payment, payable on all land to all farmers, including those who had received nothing under the previous policy regime, subject to various environmental and regulatory conditions.

What the government was effectively saying to farmers was, 'Here's an annual payment, to reward you for looking after the countryside and being an important part of the fabric of rural society. It's up to you what you use it for, but we certainly don't expect you necessarily to carry on producing food. We're no longer interested in food security or the balance of payments. We're happy to leave the level of production to be decided by the market.'

This sent two messages to the farming community. The first was that their traditional role as food producers was no longer valued. The second -- although this has taken rather longer to sink in – was that unless a food production enterprise like a dairy or beef herd was profitable in its own right, then the farmer would be better off not bothering with it.

Now the sad economic facts of the matter are that the majority of farms in Devon are not profitable if you leave the single payment out of the equation. According to a report produced by the University of Exeter's Centre for Rural Research[2] on the *Impact* of CAP Reform on Devon's Agriculture, the average lowland cattle and sheep farm in the county made a profit of just £33 per hectare (ha) in the three years 2000-02. That included the benefit of production subsidies worth £153/ha. Take those out of the equation – which is essentially what de-coupling has done – and you are left with a loss of £120/ha.

To put it another way, the average cattle and sheep farmer on 120ha of lowland Devon would be better off to the tune of £14,400 if he shut down his beef and sheep enterprises. The position with the upland livestock farms on Dartmoor and Exmoor is not quite so bad – a net loss of £32/ha – but the lesson is the same, as indeed it is for the relatively few predominantly arable farms in Devon. With wheat at £85/tonne, most of those would not be profitable without being propped up by the single payment. The position with dairy farms is slightly different, in that it was only in 2005, as de-coupling was applied, that direct payments were introduced as compensation for cuts in the support price. But even with that, some 65% of dairy farms are estimated to be operating at a loss. The conclusion is inescapable: most farmers in Devon would be better off not producing food.

Of course, it isn't quite as simple as that. There are tax complications for a start, and to make a complete withdrawal from productive agriculture make sense economically, you need

(2) *Lobley M. and Butler A. (2004)* The Impact of the CAP reform on Devon's Agriculture Final Report to Devon County Council, *Centre for Rural Research, University of Exeter.*

to be able to shed so-called fixed costs like labour, buildings and machinery. Unless and until the opportunity arises to do that, then provided a production enterprise is covering the variable costs – feed, seed, fertilisers, etc. – attributed to it, then the cash that it generates will be needed by the business.

Besides, just because a production enterprise is not profitable now does not mean it may not become profitable in the future. Farms are no more immune from the ebb and flow of supply and demand, profit and loss, than any other sort of business. Most farmers are in it for the long term, and will battle on through the inevitable troughs of farming fortunes phlegmatically enough provided they can see a reasonable prospect of returning to profit eventually.

But is there such a prospect? That is the 64,000 dollar question. The sector where production subsidies contributed the greatest proportion of total income, and which is therefore at greatest risk from their effective abolition, is beef. According to figures from the English Beef and Lamb Executive (Eblex), beef prices to the farmer would need to increase by almost 40% for extensive grass-fed beef systems, of the type to which farms in Devon are most suited, to become profitable. And whilst beef prices did rise steadily through 2006 by around 15%, I know of no one prepared to forecast a rise of anything like 40%, especially given the increased access at lower tariffs that will certainly be offered to South American beef when the world trade talks are eventually concluded (as they will be).

According to the economists at Eblex and elsewhere, the farmers most likely to achieve the Holy Grail of single payment-free profitability are the largest, most efficient and most intensive ones, and that goes for all sectors, not just beef. Devon is a county of family farms, and our landscape does not lend itself to intensive large-scale crop production any more than our rainy climate and lack of access to cheap arable by-products lends itself to large-scale, intensive livestock production. Put all of that together with the disillusionment brought on by low incomes, the ever-rising tide of red tape and regulation, the continuing misery caused by bovine tuberculosis, a sense of self-worth damaged by media criticism and perceived government hostility, and the fact that the non-farming economy is relatively buoyant and offers plenty of alternatives to the drudgery of unprofitable, unappreciated farming, and the prospects for agriculture in Devon look anything but rosy.

So what does all of this mean for the county, its economy, its countryside and its people? Well, if there is one lesson that shines out from the history of farming in Devon, it is that the farmers of this country are a tenacious lot who will not be easily uprooted from their native earth. The message from that Exeter University study of the social impact of agricultural business change is that farmers are not about to be rushed into making radical changes to their businesses and lifestyles. The prevailing mood is one of wait and see.

Besides, the advent of single payments and the new environmental schemes – which are intended to reward good land management and address environmental issues – gives farmers options. The fact that they do not have to work themselves into the ground producing food at below the cost of production has provided farmers with some genuine leverage in the supply chains of which they are part. One of the strongest trends in the marketplace is towards foods that are different, special and local: foods that by their very nature cannot be displaced by cheaper imports. Demand for organic food is rising strongly. Such is the shortage of organic milk that Asda is having to import all of its supplies, and at a recent conference in Cullompton, a senior manager from Tesco predicted that organic beef's share of sales would grow from 3% to 10% within five years.

Of course, price is still a hugely powerful driver. But as people spend a lower and lower proportion of their disposable income on food, so they can afford to be more and more choosey. Devon – with its strong associations with good things to eat and drink – is as well placed as anywhere to capitalise on this trend, and if the local food market is still relatively small, it is growing fast.

What might be called the 'environmental market' is also booming. Defra's new Entry Level and Higher Level Stewardship schemes have got off to a stuttering start, due mainly to computerised mapping systems that proved to be totally inadequate for the task in hand. But when the technical gremlins are eventually evicted from the system, there is every reason to believe – based on experience in the pilot area, near Tiverton – that take-up will be around 75% of eligible land. Payments of £60/ha for organic land and £30/ha for other land may not represent a king's ransom, but they will be a useful supplement to whatever other income the farmer can earn, and – unlike previous agri-environment schemes – they will be available to all. One thing that we can say for certain is that there will be significantly more of Devon being consciously managed for environmental benefit in the future than there has been in the past.

Markets for non-food outputs are booming as well. Whether it is farm tourism, or barn conversions, or warehousing, or small-scale food processing, there is money to be made from it if you are in the right place and have the right skills and aptitudes. Ironically, the key to success for the diversified elements of farming will be a healthy core business. Because if we can achieve that, then farmers will be diversifying from choice rather than desperation, and the danger of these new markets being swamped will be greatly reduced.

One of the best things about the new regime is that young people trying to start or develop their farming businesses will no longer have to overcome the huge obstacle of land costs inflated by the subsidy regime. We are already seeing land becoming available, at little or no rent, from those who decide to take the option provided by single payments of maintaining ownership of the land and claiming single payment on it, but allowing someone else to farm it. I am convinced that the mainstream business of food production will increasingly and probably fairly rapidly be concentrated in the hands of those who are good at it, who are prepared to work hard at it and who enjoy what they do, and very many of those people will be under the age of 40.

The successful farm businesses of the future will be those operated by farmers who are focused on their markets, who make best use of information technology, particularly in coping with the regulatory burden, and who are prepared to collaborate not only in marketing, but in sharing labour and machinery and, perhaps most of all, in acquiring and using knowledge.

The other change that I am hoping for is that, as the baleful influence of politics recedes, so the true value of farming will once again be understood and appreciated. It is often said that you don't know what you've got until it's gone, and that was certainly true of foot and mouth disease. That experience left many farmers disillusioned and traumatised, but it also helped many others to a deeper understanding of why they had become farmers in the first place. In my survey an immensely encouraging 35% said that it had reinforced their determination and desire to be livestock farmers.

More than that, the pent-up emotions that it released produced an almost cathartic outpouring of poetry, prose, drama, music and painting that has greatly enriched our understanding of the deep and complex relationships between the farmer, his animals, the land and the natural world. And what is perhaps most encouraging is that this cultural renaissance in Devon farming does not appear to have been a nine-day wonder. Thanks to individuals like Peter and Suzanne Redstone, with their *Art Farm* Festivals, and organisations like Aune Head Arts, there has been a veritable explosion of artistic endeavour on and about farms, right across the region.

So my conclusion is a relatively optimistic one. In historical terms, we are moving from an era of stability into one of uncertainty. The security of political protection is being stripped away, leaving farmers exposed to the vagaries of market forces. The consequences for the business of food production may very well be difficult and damaging in the short term.

But, as Francis Bacon long ago observed, *"Adversity doth best discover virtue"*, and I have no doubt that, over time, a younger, more dynamic, more entrepreneurial and more self-confident farming industry will emerge, that is more in tune with the times and with its customers. Yes, it will probably be smaller, but that need not mean that vast swathes of the countryside go to rack and ruin. Thanks to the various environmental schemes, the vast majority of Devon will continue to be managed, even if, for the time being at least, rather less of it is farmed.

As for the farmers themselves, well, in Devon, history suggests that they are conservative by choice, resourceful by necessity and tenacious to a remarkable degree. It is a combination that should stand them – and the entire county – in good stead as we face the challenge of making the most of the new world of farming without letting go of the best of the past.

Anthony Gibson *was born in Totnes in 1949 and has lived most of his life in Devon. He read history at Oxford before joining the NFU in 1972 as a speech-writer and in-house journalist. He served as regional director for the NFU in the South West from 1992 until his appointment as NFU Director of Communications in 2006, and led the farming industry in the region through both the BSE and foot and mouth crises. He was appointed OBE for services to agriculture and the rural economy in the South West in the 2003 Queen's Birthday Honours.*

Further reading: Silence at Ramscliffe, *Chris Chapman and James Crowden, Bardwell Press, Oxford, 2005 ;* The History of Devonshire: From the Earliest Period to the Present, *(3 Vols) Rev. Thomas Moore, Robert Jennings, London, 1829–1836.*

Farmed by Trudy
& Andrew Hawkins
Artwork by Tessa Bunney
& Louise Cottey

Louise Cottey

Louise's creations were, literally, intertwined with the farm; each made with materials found within a few yards of where she placed them. These video images (above) of the work in situ are taken from documentation of the project.

"A metaphor for the relationship [between artist and farmer] might be found in Louise Cottey's visual constructions offering small fragments of farm life – sheep wool, feathers, baler twine and black plastic – caught like thoughts in the fences surrounding the farm. Tiny and poignant in the vast Exmoor landscape, these re-workings of ordinary debris on the edges of farmland seem to suggest the fragile beginning of a new interface: a connection between farmers and the rest of us, through the voice of the artist."

From Jennie Hayes, 'Field Work'.

Dartmoor to the Earl of Cornwall in 1239 and William IV sold Exmoor to a Midlands entrepreneur called Knight in the early-nineteenth century. Dartmoor's owner became the Duke, the dukedom reverted to the heir to the throne and, despite enclosure round the edges and along the turnpikes that crossed it, its 'forest' heart remained open. It became common land

In order to exhibit the weavings, each had to be removed from its setting – bolt cutters taken to these fragile reflections of farm activity. The pieces were woven into the fabric of the exhibition to replicate the experience of discovering them when on site at Warren Farm. Here you see a small weaving placed behind the television monitors at the exhibition in Buckland Abbey.

proper only in 1970. The Knight family, moving their entrepreneurial skill into agriculture, attempted to reclaim Exmoor's 'forest' from 1820 on, and largely succeeded round the edges and up the valleys. They created new farmsteads and wanted mile upon mile of beech-topped hedge-bank as shelter for new enclosures. The Hawkins live in a 'Knight' farm carved out

As an honorary family member during her residency, Louise involved the Hawkins children in her work. They learned to card wool, the difference between warp and weft, and how different materials behave.

of the Exmoor 'forest' soon after 1820. The farmstead lies halfway up the valley side facing south, opposite Exe Cleave. It is the last farm upstream in the highest reach of the River Exe, perhaps 3 miles from Exe Head and just a mile and a half north-east of Simonsbath. At 383m OD, Warren Farm is the highest home of our farming families, and while the Hawkins

Weaving on wire fence. Experiment in dying techniques and the effects of weathering.

61

are freeholders, like their Dartmoor colleagues they have grazing on a large single area of moorland – some 2,400 acres of the erstwhile Exmoor Forest which abuts the farm. It is not common, but a huge enclosure of which they are the sole tenants, their landlord being the National Park Authority. Warren Farm was purchased from the Exmoor National Park in

the Hawkins family – Andrew, Trudy and children Richard (14 at the time of the *Focus on Farmers* project), Giles (12), Hannah (10) and Rebecca (8). The farm has no mains electricity and its own water supply, making it one of the most isolated farms on Exmoor. Warren Farm is a traditional, family-run Exmoor hill farm, the only farm of our four situated in Somerset,

Tessa Bunney

< Twenty folding chairs upholstered in hunting fabric were a functional as well as an artistic part of the exhibitions. Tessa was drawn to using same material as in the Hawkins' dining-room curtains as it evoked the family's commitment to horses and hunting. The same material was also used to cover Tessa's book *Growing up with Horses*.

"Focus on Farmers has enabled me realise a lot about my working practice – that although I usually work alone to produce my work, my relationship with the people I am photographing is the most important factor to its success. Your working process is a very personal thing so it has been interesting to step back and see how the way I work might be viewed by another artist and vice versa. It is always interesting to see how a different artist picks up on different issues and sees the same place and people very differently through their work. I feel we have been open about our working processes with each other and the farm – something which artists are not always renowned for!"

Tessa Bunney, from mid-project evaluation, August 2003

63

working with beef cattle and sheep. The family also run a bed and breakfast business. The river Exe runs down the southern Warren valley, and north of the farm the land borders the Doone Valley, made famous by R.D. Blackmore's *Lorna Doone*, in which the farm is mentioned.

Each of these photographs was blown up to 24 x 24 inches for exhibition. As each image was unframed, viewing them was more like looking through a window onto these scenes on and around the farm than at something static.

Growing up with Horses

Tessa Bunney

Tessa wrote in her mid-term report:

"The Hawkins family are 'horse mad' – riding, point to point, pony club, hunting are all part of their daily life – these are aspects to farming which I have previously not had any involvement with personally or professionally. It has been interesting to look at these activities from the 'inside', what it is to have a passion for horses – the whole family have ridden since early childhood."

In response to the Hawkins family passion, Tessa created the book entitled *Growing up with Horses,* capturing an engagement with horses which extended beyond the Hawkins family and across the local community.

"My parents have always had point to pointers and it's what a lot of country people do for a sport because it's part and parcel of where you live. It's something I really enjoy, good fun, the children like riding and it's something we can do as a family." Extract from *Growing up with Horses.*

THANK YOU FOR
SHOPPING AT
OTTAKAR'S

Field Work
Jennie Hayes
Collaboration and dialogue in Focus on Farmers

"Vision that responds to the cries of the world and is truly engaged with what it sees is not the same as the disembodied eye that observes and reports, that objectifies and enframes. The ability to enter into another's emotions, or to share another's plight, to make their conditions our own, characterizes art in the partnership mode. You cannot exactly define it as self-expression – it is more like relational dynamics."
Suzi Gablik[1]

How should farmers farm?
Douglas Harper's book, *Changing Works: Visions of a Lost Agriculture*, provides a fascinating overview of how dairy farming in upstate New York is changing fast with the onset of technology and industrialised labour. Asking ecological and timely questions about the social and cultural importance of agriculture, he poses the question, 'What is it to farm?'. As if in response, Jan Wojcik writes:

"How should farmers farm? From time immemorial there has been really one answer. Farmers should farm so that they can farm again".[2]

I am fascinated by this succinct and meaningful interpretation, although as Harper notes, its simplicity belies the complexity of the question. We are living in a culture of spending and expendability. In arts and farming alike, over many years, too little thought has been given to long-term investment in our culture and agriculture. Shifting policies have influenced practices for better or worse. Separatist approaches have further removed the reality of creative and agricultural production from our daily lives. Meat is packaged in germ-free plastic in our supermarkets. Art is sealed behind the glass doors of too-scary galleries. Through their finish, both conceal the reality of production.

72

(1) *Gablik S. (1991)* The Reenchantment of Art, *London: Thames & Hudson. p106*

(2) *Wojcik J. quoted in Harper D. (2001)* Changing Works: Visions of a Lost Agriculture, *London: University of Chicago Press. p278*

The Common Agricultural Policy changed the nature of our farming practices and therefore our countryside. Cultural policies around capital planning, exhibition, performance and management practices have defined how the arts are seen (and not seen) in our society. We are reaping the results, with a too-late eye to sustainability.

The connections between arts and agriculture are implicitly identified through *Focus on Farmers*, accompanying the invitation for the artist to explore the farming homestead. Whilst the parallel between the two is not the subject of this essay, I am intrigued by the opportunities for dialogue and relationships enabled through the exploration of farming via the arts.

The artist as stranger

The farming homestead, perhaps, is unique. The home provides the life-blood for the family *and* the business. There is, by necessity, little separation of roles – the transition between the two imperceptible and fluid. It is also entirely reliant on its location, its acreage of land, its complexity of farm buildings. The land and location *is* the business and is also the site of nurturing for the family. Any risks or mistakes affect it all.

Into this complex cultural location comes a stranger. Not any old stranger, but one charged with documenting the lives of those within. One charged with asking awkward questions, with looking at those lives in a different way,

with re-presenting those lives to a wider public. Not any old stranger, but an artist. And not just one artist, but two.

Is it possible for these interlopers to share in an already complex working-living-playing-caring business-home environment? What happens when an artist attempts to make work in this midst: work which is not separate and removed but engaged and embedded in the life of the farm?

What happens when...?

I became involved in *Focus on Farmers* because I'm interested in what happens when artists and (so-called) non-artists come together in arts projects. Whose story is being told and why? Who has the power? How does it affect the work? What are the principles by which artists work in this context and how do they differ from other kinds of projects? Is it worth doing?

I was interested in how relationships might develop in this intense situation which could influence both the way in which work was made and how the final product looked. I was curious at the approach of Aune Head Arts, who had created neither a community arts project nor a straightforward artist-in-residence event. I wondered at the refreshing openness of a brief which was designed to offer the artists creative freedom yet demanded something which might offer a glimpse to a wider audience. I was particularly interested in a project which set so much store on the development of *relationships* between artists

73

and farmers and yet refused to determine or predict how those relationships might develop in relation to the artists' role on the farm. Instead, Aune Head Arts provided a supportive, practical framework which ensured the close proximity of artists to the farming families through the bed and breakfast arrangements, regular dinner events and continual dialogue, rather than a brief which restricted or demanded a particular role of the artist in that context.

It felt like a scenario fraught with tension, with problems waiting to arise. I found myself, when interviewing those involved, looking for where things had gone wrong and where the intensity of the relationship had revealed itself in word or deed or in the final work.

I discovered that there were indeed tense moments, but the level of trust and consideration that had to be developed due to the co-dependent nature of the relationship contributed not, for the most part, to a fraught working environment, but to one where increased understandings informed the development of the arts practices taking place. This relationship itself began to create the potential for new ways of working for the artists involved.

I was interested in how the artists might deal with the 'bloody' part of farming: the slaughter, the killing shed, the hunt. I found a level of understanding within the artists' process of working and the work itself which neither sensationalised nor avoided those

issues. The complexity of the relationship with life and death is reflected in poetry, striving not to make simplistic political statements but to allow the result of the new dialogue to emerge.

The farmhand
explains how turkey blood runs red
out of the slaughtering shed
into the adjacent piece of ground –

a river of food
on a farm – where life is as normal as death.

(Lifelines (extract), Tania van Schalkwyk
June 2003: Kestor Way, Chagford, Devon.)

And Beth Hamer, as a farmer's daughter, hunt saboteur and artist, was able to confront contentious political issues through good-natured dialogue with her host family. Whether either shifted in view is irrelevant: if *"…meaning is created intersubjectively, between people who are in some way or another in touch with one another…"*,[3] then the opportunities for the creation of new meaning are supported and engendered by such a project, leading to the possibilities, over

(3) *Hylland Eriksen T. (1993)* Symbolic power struggles in inter-cultural space. *Lecture delivered at the symposium "Culture in the Global Village", Lund, Sweden, 14–16 January, 1993.* Published in Swedish in Oscar Hemer, ed., Kulturen i den globala byn, *Ægis 1994. http://folk.uio.no/geirthe/Symbolic. html accessed 14 June 2005.*

a long period of time, for positive outcomes in our relationships with one another and with the world.

The resulting work comprises no artist's objective outside eye, and it is not the relatively clear and uncomplicated perspective that might be offered by a farmer either. It is an eye shadowed by merging boundaries, softened by new information and jarred by conflicting emotions. It is the product of a collaboration.

Power and context

There are a number of ways in which a project such as this might be driven, shaped and defined. Projects which involve 'members of the public' could be community or participatory arts, education projects, artists in residence, community development projects, socially engaged practices or documentation projects, for example.

In a climate of government policy around social inclusion and education, we have become accustomed to projects where the expectation is that the artist will offer something to the community in order that the community can make something for themselves. There is pressure on these kinds of projects to make claims around transformation and social change, often involving the measuring of social targets.[4]

Focus on Farmers made no claims to either.

I was refreshed by the lack of social targets to the *Focus on Farmers* project. Instead, this project operated with a genuine intent to reflect the lives of South West hill farmers, alongside a keen sense of artistic integrity and sensitivity in relation to how the artists and farmers might live and work together.

Integrating artists in communities always brings with it issues of power and equality. Whilst an artist might assume or hope for an equal dialogue (and not all do), they bring with them a knowledge, skills base and level of control over the product which inevitably weights the power in their favour. Even in situations where it is the 'community's' story that is to be told, the artist, certainly initially, usually holds the reigns, if on behalf of an invisible stakeholder or funder. This is in part due to our cultural placing of artists as 'other'. As a society we tend towards an obstinate refusal to understand 'The Arts', yet, paradoxically, we revere and desire the 'artist as genius' as part of our social make-up.

We nurture an elitist view of the arts which, whilst paying lip service to education and 'arts for all', acknowledges the true validity only of particular kinds of artistic production created within established frameworks.

In the case of *Focus on Farmers*, I was

75

(4) *Arts Council England states in* Ambitions for the Arts *2003: 2–3 "It is our central belief that the arts have power to transform lives, communities and opportunities for people throughout the country. We will argue that being involved with the arts can have a lasting and transforming effect on many aspects of people's lives. This is true not just for individuals, but also for neighbourhoods, communities, regions and entire generations, whose sense of identity and purpose can be changed through art".*

intrigued at how, because of the location, the brief, the integrity and sensitivity of the artists involved and the strength of the identity of the 'participants' (the farming families), it appeared possible that, in some cases, the power relationship had been turned upside down.

The artists were not on home territory or in a dedicated arts space (arts centre, gallery, theatre, etc). For part of the time they were not even going home at night. Their work had to fit into the pattern of the farmers' daily lives. There was, by necessity, little concession to artists' routines or working practices. Some did not have obvious opportunities to share their work in progress with the families. Some felt uncomfortable with the issues they had to deal with on a daily basis. There was some difficulty for the artists in finding ways to 'offer' their expertise in a context that was necessarily busy, purposeful and, in some cases, where the farmers were often not as interested in their arts partners as the artists were in them. After all, although everyone had chosen to take part, this was an arts project, initiated by an arts organisation, not by the farming community.

Despite this, the risks inherent in the project were as great for the farmers as the artists. Who might imagine what the stranger in their midst might do?

A metaphor for the relationship might be found in Louise Cottey's visual constructions offering small fragments of farm life – sheep wool, feathers, baler twine and black plastic – caught like thoughts in the fences surrounding the farm. Tiny and poignant in the vast Exmoor landscape, these re-workings of ordinary debris on the edges of farmland seem to suggest the fragile beginning of a new interface: a connection between farmers and the rest of us, through the voice of the artist.

The right to choose

In observing this project I am reminded of Jean Mohr's description of photographing the mountain farmer 'Marcel'. Marcel had strong views on how people should be photographed, presumably in response to Mohr's images. (*"If you take a head, you should take the whole head, the whole head and shoulders. Not just a part of the face."*)[5]. One Sunday, Mohr arrived to find Marcel dressed, in contrast to his working gear, in a clean ironed black shirt, with a shaved face and combed hatless head. Mohr writes:

"When he saw this portrait, in which he had chosen everything for himself, he said with a kind of relief: 'And now my grandchildren will know what sort of man I was.'"[6]

By controlling, as well as he could, his own representation, Marcel began an unspoken dialogue with the artist which produced an image entirely from that collaboration. Mohr called the piece, *Marcel or the Right*

(5) *Berger J. and Mohr J. (1982)* Another Way of Telling *London: Writers & Readers Publishing Cooperative Society. p23.*
(6) *Berger J. and Mohr J. (1982)* Another Way of Telling *pp36-37.*

to Choose. The 'subject' disrupted the artist's preconception of his image-making by offering a presentation of himself which was then embraced and worked on by the artist. The artist's openness and reflection enabled the image (and its surrounding analysis) to offer a new story, beyond documentary and incorporating multiple voices.

This notion of collaboration highlights the need for the artist to be conscious and questioning of their own viewpoint, to continually challenge and reflect upon their own agendas and motives. As Marsha Meskimmon writes, drawing on Donna Haraway's work on situated knowledges:

"...we must acknowledge the position from which we see, the particular embodiment of our own eyes, and then be both critical of our vision and accountable for it." [7]

Nowhere is this more important than when one is attempting to re-present the life of another. Immersion in the creative process can blind one to the obvious fact of our vision. The work remains that of the artist, without a doubt, but the voice of the farmer can be heard within it. It emerges from a dialogue, in some cases explicitly, as in Gregg Wagstaff's interviews with the Malseed family and Tony Hill and Hannah Standen's conversations with Arnold and Bridget Cole. In other cases the dialogue is more subtle, as in Kirsty Waterworth and Beth Hamer's use of the Coakers' farm identification number in installation and Tessa Bunney's examination of the role of horses within the Hawkins family. In all cases the artist has been involved in a process of making which is informed, on a daily basis, not only by the context of the farmstead but by the voices of the farming families.

The level of immersion by the artist in the daily life of the farm was perhaps one of the greatest successes of *Focus on Farmers*. Some artists expressed desire for even more immersion; others found themselves surprisingly challenged by the length of the residency.[8] It enabled the artists to develop a relationship which both challenged the nature of the work (and their working practices) and informed their presentation. The artist became complicit in farming life; minding children, erecting fences, rounding up cattle, accompanying the hunt, eating family meals, drinking tea, using the kitchen table. As Kirsty Waterworth wrote in her mid-project report, *"By throwing myself into the farm and people, I have been more a participant than an observer."*

This was no simple 'witnessing' of events by an artist; the artist knelt to weave sheep wool

(7) Meskimmon M. (1996) The Art of Reflection: Women's Artists' Self-Portraiture in the Twentieth Century, *London: Scarlet Press. p9*

(8) *The brief for the project specified that the artist should work for 30 days on the project (thereby sleeping over for 30 nights). Each artist split this 30-day period into shorter time-spans, the longest being two sessions of two weeks each.*

with farming children, caused a stir with her urban beauty at the farmers' market, wrapped herself up on the baling machine and got out of bed to find the lamb already slaughtered. Conversely, the farmer took a walk across the fields recording with a mini-disk and told stories for the website. The farmer's daughter wrote poetry.

The boundaries are not fixed between artist and farmer, observer and observed, storymaker and storyteller. A sensitive approach on behalf of the artist reflects concerns that investigate the dynamics between place and people, history and context, power and relationships. A dialogic approach to arts work doesn't deny the voice of the artist (how could it?) and instead experiments with the creative possibilities emerging from relationships between time, people, place and ideas. The artist does not (and cannot) pretend to hide in this relationship; neither can they forget their deep responsibility and indebtedness to their collaborators. It's part of what Suzi Gablik calls "*relational dynamics.*"[9]

So, did the farmers, like Marcel, have the 'right to choose'? Like any true creative process, the outcome was always uncertain and the process itself threw up daily decisions, conscious and unconscious.

I imagined how the farming families might 'present' their world to the artist in ways parallel to, but less obvious than, donning a best shirt and combing their hair. The future of farming in this early twenty-first century is uncertain. Farmers have more at stake than simply looking smart, which in any case owes as much to a view of our relationship to photography as it does to a wider concern about how we communicate stories about our lives.

If the 'presentation' by the farming families might in itself be interpreted as problematic for the artist hoping to re-present an authentic and 'pure' experience of contemporary hill farming, it does, in my view, comprise part of the dialogue which forms the context for working and is a significant contribution to the creative process. It is part of the complexity of a residency attempting to tell a story which is not (wholly) the artist's own. If there is frustration felt on behalf of the artist, then this is part of the collaborative process. And the success of the collaborative process is evidenced by the development of trust and respect between the collaborators, which impacts on both the way of working and the end product. Another kind of artist might call it compromise.

If this 'presentation' makes invisible some aspects of farm life, it makes visible a different kind of dialogue through the cluttered space between the farmers' and the artists' voices. The 'not-seen' is replaced by a newly shaped story emerging from a complex and evolving relationship. If there are visual 'moments' which identify the extent of this new relationship they might include the unlikely picture of an

(9) *Gablik S. (1991)* The Reenchantment of Art, *London: Thames & Hudson. p106*

old Devon farmer giving a daughterly hug to a young sound artist; of the farmer genuinely problem-solving the incongruous hanging of a chandelier in a disused barn; and the filmmaker revealing his blisters after having spent a day erecting fencing.

How should artists make art?

Crucial to the success of this piece of work were the values inherent in the process of working, the negotiation between artists and participants/collaborators and the intention of the work being a touchstone for the successful and inclusive progress of the piece. Each artist entered a period of negotiation and had utmost concern for the voice of the farming family within the work. Just as her role as a researcher is expressed by Roz Hall, each artist located her/himself, *"...as one who was finding out rather than as one who knew"*. [10]

A dialogic approach to arts production is one that complicates and renders problematic the myth of the clear, unadulterated voice of the artist, of the artist as outsider and of the objective eye. It doesn't necessarily say 'everyone is an artist' (why should we assume that everyone desires to be an artist?), but that everyone can find different ways to become 'speakers' in our society through a variety of means, including arts practice. It's different but

equally valuable. It's not about 'giving' people a voice (if that were even possible), but about finding different ways to encourage the rest of us to listen.

Aune Head Arts has a practice which sensitively negotiates a series of creative relationships across Devon and beyond, allowing space to 'see what happens' when the impact of an artist's collaboration is felt. A vital element of the success of *Focus on Farmers* was that Aune Head Arts has a *long-term* commitment to its main constituency – people living and working on Dartmoor, including artists. Because of this they provide a framework that ensures local accountability and relevance of any initiative and provides an informed expert context for the artists. The company's work is predicated on trust and the building of long-term sustainable relationships with their neighbours across Dartmoor. The work of Aune Head Arts, and others like it, endeavours to cut against the trend of separatism and commodification of the arts and instead values the processes and contexts of working.

I will leave it to others, more expert than I, to determine a strategy for sustainable farming. But a manifesto for sustainable art making might endeavour to advocate that *how* we make art is just as important as the art we make. It might help us regain the connections between art and the rest of our lives. It might include investment in developing the role of artists embedded in our communities, as

(10) *Hall R. (2003) Developing Forms of Democratic Evaluation presented at* Artist as Educator Interrupt seminar *12th/13th May 2003, Ikon Gallery and University of Central England reproduced at www.interrupt-symposia.org/*

valued and committed dialogists and long-term collaborators. It might develop more meaningful learning and training opportunities for artists, including those in higher education, to ensure their ongoing active reflection and development of relevant skills to work in community settings. Crucially, it would find ways to value the cultural processes and contexts and produce of people of all social and cultural backgrounds, not just that produced by an educated elite, within a commodity culture. Finally, it would include a genuine attempt on behalf of arts practitioners to find ways to properly engage locally and meaningfully, as artists or simply as citizens.

And this returns me to Jan Wojkik's view of how farmers should farm. Artists who open themselves up to creative dialogue with people who were once but might no longer be strangers, who are not afraid of the notion of service as part of their artistic integrity, who have a genuine desire to take perhaps unfashionable risks with their practice (long after the notion of socially engaged practice comes and goes again), might come round to the same simple outcome: artists should make art so that they can make art again.

80

Jennie Hayes is a writer, photographer and arts manager. She was AHRB Research Fellow in Creative and Performing Arts at Dartington College of Arts between 2002 and 2005. She observed the Focus on Farmers *project and interviewed artists and farmers as part of an action research project.*

C is for... Simon Timms

"I don't understand it. Why do them want to 'eave me out? I've never wanted to 'eave out anyone in my life."

You don't often expect to see a Westcountry farmer cry. Or at least you didn't before 2001 – the year that the government's crisis response to the foot and mouth outbreak brought such chaos and suffering to so many local farming families.

Prior to 2001, the memory of two farmers in tears has left a particular mark in my mind. The first was a Cornish farmer with a small dairy farm, as he realised that his investment (supported by a large bank loan) in a spanking new milking parlour had backfired, a victim of sudden changes to milk quotas.

The second was the Devon farmer quoted at the start of this chapter, who was being forced ("*'eaved out*", in his words) from his family farm to make way for a new reservoir. It would bring boundless water to tens of thousands of residents and visitors but cause forced eviction for his family. To see him standing with tears running down his cheeks as the bulldozers began to rip out the hedges around his farmhouse would have made a profound impression on any bystander.

Of course, today fewer and fewer people have the chance actually to meet a real farmer on a real farm, let alone see one in tears. The census of 1851 recorded for the first time that England had more urban dwellers than rural ones. And over the ensuing 150 years our unswerving march towards a more urbanised, and indeed global, society has severed the age-old links that so many people had with their local countryside.

Today the South West still has slightly more people living in small towns and rural communities than in the region's urban centres, such as Exeter, Truro and Plymouth. But only a small minority of them actually live and work in the real countryside. It should be no surprise to find that, according to government figures, fewer than 10,000 of the South West's population of almost five million are paid-up members of the National Farmers' Union. The farming industry now accounts for less than 2.5% of the region's GDP.

Perhaps the twentieth-century experience of my own family is typical of that of many over the last 100 years. Both my parents grew up during the opening decades of the twentieth century on very small Westcountry farms. Their own parents supplemented what they could make as tenant farmers by working as rabbit catchers and odd-jobbers on neighbouring estates.

One of my mother's most vivid childhood memories was of selling eggs and butter (and, in season, buying mazzards) at the weekly Barnstaple Pannier Market during the war years (First World War, that is). There she saw her customers' clothing turn blacker and sadder as more and more families went into mourning dress to mark the loss of a son or a father. My father proudly won a prize as a teenager in the local ploughing competition. But by then he had already made up his mind to leave the farm as soon as he could get enough education inside him to find work elsewhere.

As a result, my childhood experience of agricultural life was limited to the visits back to the old family farm in the summer holidays to witness the abundance of the harvest. And my children, growing up in the last quarter of the twentieth century, enjoyed an even more restricted view of the working countryside. They had the odd day out or the occasional school visit to a farm, where seeing a live chicken for the first time was a memorable experience for some of their classmates.

This ever-growing trend that has divorced (yes it is truly the end of a long-term relationship) so many of us from any genuine year-round connection with farming has been matched with profound changes in the way in which the countryside is being farmed – or 'managed' to use the increasingly common word.

Change in rural life is, of course, nothing new. Some 120 years ago that most prolific of

Devon authors the Rev. Sabine Baring Gould, in his Devon novel, *Red Spider* (1887, pp v-vi) informed his readers that he was writing about:

" … sundry pictures of what was beginning to fade half a century ago in Devon. Old customs, modes of thought, of speech, quaint sayings, weird superstitions are all disappearing out of the country utterly for ever. The labourer is now enfranchised, education is universal, railways have made life circulate freer; and we stand now before a great social dissolving view, from which old things are passing away and what is coming on we can only partly guess, but not wholly distinguish."

And rural change has been ever present way back beyond the nineteenth century. Local historians have shown that the traditional view that farming families in past centuries stayed put throughout their generations in the same parish is too simplistic.

Some certainly did (and Devon was perhaps known more than other counties as a place where people led 'stationary' lives). The Seccombe family, for example, lived at the same West Devon farm from the thirteenth century through to the end of the twentieth century. Their farm was even named Seccombe after them (or vice versa). And the Seccombes won first prize at the Devon County Show in the 1970s for being the longest established Devon farming family.

And then there were the Sokespitches,

such ancient scions of Devon that they viewed the Courtenays, living in splendour nearby at Powderham Castle, as mere upstarts. According to W.G. Hoskins, writing in his *Old Devon* (1966, pp 121-134) the Sokespitches lived on the same farm beside the River Clyst (doing very little it seems) for over 600 years from the 1170s through to 1803. Then, in a moment of *"fatal disturbance of the spirit"*, they cut their roots and disappeared off to India.

But for many sons and daughters of farmers through the centuries, moving away from their home parish to pastures new was a not uncommon experience. These migrations were paralleled by changes in settlement patterns as rural places expanded into hamlets and then shrank back to being single farms again, or even became completely deserted.

In one of his splendid academic explorations of medieval settlements in Devon, Professor Harold Fox has opened our eyes to the dynamic oscillations that the far-flung north Devon manor of Hartland went through in the Middle Ages. From surviving medieval documents, he revealed that its hamlets had declined into isolated farmsteads and even fallen off the map completely. Yet visitors to Hartland today can easily be misled into thinking that they are looking at an unchanged ancient landscape, reaching back to time immemorial.

So it would be wrong to view change in the countryside as anything new. But the increasing rate of change in the twentieth century has brought with it several elements that distinguish modern trends from those witnessed by previous generations. I will focus on just three of these areas of change here.

The loss of working farms

Firstly, modern change has seen more and more farmsteads – some occupying sites that have housed farmers since the Domesday Book, or even going back to Roman and prehistoric times – ceasing to be farmed as they are put to other uses.

Take for example, Old Bridwell. Dating back to at least 1280, this Devon farmstead found itself, in the 1980s, caught up in the modern trend of conversion from working farm to a cluster of cosy dwellings (with *"disastrous alterations"*, according to Pevsner's and Cherry's Devon volume in the *Buildings of England* series). Thus no longer can you see the names and parting messages of Victorian farm labourers scribbled in pencil on the whitewashed barn wall on the eve of their departure to Canada to seek a better life. Today these walls are adorned with the latest style of kitchen unit.

Or there is the Domesday manor of Ashbury, tucked away in deepest Devon surrounded by far-flung views to both Exmoor and Dartmoor. Ashbury became a medieval parish with no village centre – just a church, manor house, and a few scattered hamlets and farmsteads. One of these farmsteads was Scobchester. Medieval documents date it back to at least 1242 but its name is redolent of a much more ancient,

possibly Roman, past, for 'chester' comes from the Latin 'castrum', meaning army camp.

Scobchester survives now just as a place name, and Ashbury House itself was demolished in 1934. The parish church, too, has become redundant (although still wonderfully cared for and open to visitors). Most recently, the old home farm and its extensive outbuildings beside the church have been converted into a number of well-appointed dwellings – creating today's non-agricultural equivalent of the rural hamlet that was at the heart of medieval farming life in this part of Devon.

These two random examples highlight a trend that is becoming increasingly common. English Heritage has recently analysed this trend in the South West and found that over 30% of farmstead buildings which are listed as being of historic interest have been converted to other uses. In South Devon, a particularly good hunting ground for second home buyers, the conversion rate tops 50%.

One of the side effects of this trend is that traditional farmsteads cared for by large estates or conservation bodies are now increasingly being viewed as something like museum pieces. Some are being deliberately preserved. Thus the Dartmoor National Park Authority has purchased Higher Uppacott, a medieval longhouse in Widecombe in the Moor parish, with the express intention of preserving this moorland longhouse tradition.

Alongside the conversion of traditional buildings has been the appetite we have nourished over the last 50 years for building homes and factories in the countryside. This growth of 'greenfield' development has only very recently been slowed down by a change of government policy. This is not before greenfield development has been allowed to run rampant in some parts of the country. According to government figures, the value of good farmland can shoot up from under £10,000 per hectare to over £2.2 million per hectare the moment that the local council has granted planning permission for residential development.

This English trend is a direct result of the increasing urbanisation of our society – something that is being mirrored around the world. In China it is happening on a staggering scale. Media reports state that, according to the Chinese government, in 2005 alone 6.7 million hectares of Chinese farmland were put over to urban development, leaving 30 million farmers without land or jobs. According to a report in *The Guardian* (21 January 2006, p21), China's Ministry of Public Security has expressed concern at the social stress caused by this wholesale land seizure, which sparked off a total of 87,000 protests and demonstrations in a single year (an average of some 230 every day!).

The impact of new agricultural policy

Even where land remains in agricultural use, it is still undergoing profound change on a scale not witnessed in previous centuries. In this country, much of the change in agricultural practices is attributed to the complex and, to many people's minds, unfathomable policies brought in under the European Common Agricultural Policy.

Agricultural subsidies make up the largest allocation in the European Union's overall budget, and many farmers had come to rely on such regular subsidies. All this is now up for change. The old system, which rewarded farmers for the number of animals they stocked or the quantity of crops they grew, is being replaced by the new Single Farm Payment Scheme. This new system calculates payments on the amount and quality of land held and the environmental standards to which that land is farmed. The financial incentive to over-stock or over-produce has been removed.

These funding changes are set to have a deep impact not just on the lives of farmers but also on the environmental quality and visual appearance of the countryside. The future for small family farmers in upland landscapes is likely to be particularly challenging. Hill farms are set to attract a much reduced level of support under the new European system. Initial media reports suggest that the UK's 2005 negotiations on its European rebate may see a reduction of up to 40% in support for some areas of agriculture.

Already there are signs that fewer animals are grazing upland areas such as the Lake District. This is leaving more land exposed to the growth of scrub vegetation. There is even talk today of some areas being allowed to revert back to 'wilderness' landscape. Put the longer-term impacts of climate change alongside the results of these policy shifts and few visitors to the uplands will be left in doubt about the rate of change they see on the fells around them.

This issue was put under the spotlight by a dilemma that faced the National Trust in 2005 – what to do at High Yewdale Farm, one of its small hill farms in the Lake District. The farm tenancy at High Yewdale had fallen vacant and the Trust's financial forecasts clearly indicated that it could not continue as its own small farming unit under the new agricultural support regime. The Trust's proposal was to amalgamate the High Yewdale land with four adjacent small farms to allow these neighbouring farmers the chance to adjust better to the future. Importantly, amalgamation also would bring with it the real potential to improve the environmental management of the land in nature conservation terms, as well as safeguarding the farm's hefted flock of Herdwick sheep.

The Trust's amalgamation proposal received some strong initial criticism, not only from a local pressure group, but also in the national press. The controversy was heightened by the fact that High Yewdale had been originally given to the National Trust by the well-known children's book writer, Beatrix Potter. (It is little known that she, in her own time, had seen the need sometimes to amalgamate farms.)

In the end the Trust's decision to go ahead with the amalgamation of the High Yewdale land received support in the pages of *Country Life* and from other influential organisations. Hopefully, its Herdwicks can long continue to graze the fells untroubled by further such controversy. But the whole episode has served as a wake-up call for the agricultural industry and, hopefully, for our government. There is a crucial need now to support the role of hill farmers in managing upland landscapes if they are to provide a decent way of life for future farmers.

Growing public support for our countryside

This leads us to the third fundamental area of change that the countryside has witnessed during the twentieth century – the enormous rise in public support for our rural landscapes. Reaching back to the National Trust Act of 1907, there has been a series of advances during the last century stemming from growing public recognition of the value of the countryside.

This has resulted, for example, in increased controls over rural land use through the town and country planning legislation, accompanied by the introduction of a raft of new agri-environment management schemes. The 1950s brought the creation of national parks and also the first Areas of Outstanding Natural Beauty. This means that, according to English Heritage's *Heritage Counts 2005* publication, currently 37% of the landmass of the South West falls within some kind of designated landscape area (the figure is nearer 50% for Devon).

Public support for conserving the countryside through careful management has also been witnessed in the rapid rise in membership of such voluntary organisations as the National Trust, the Campaign to Protect Rural England, the Royal Society for the Protection of Birds and the Wildlife Trusts. The National Trust alone has seen a splendid rise in membership to 3.4 million people today.

From their outset, organisations like these have held a shared concern for caring for the countryside, its heritage, flora and fauna. They also have had another key ambition – that is the strong desire (even more relevant today) to give greater opportunity for people, particularly urban dwellers, to gain access to the countryside. The recent 'right to roam' legislation is but the latest step forward in widening public access.

This two-fold approach is well summed up by the aims of the Youth Hostel Association, founded in 1931 to *"help all, especially young people of limited means, to a greater knowledge, love and care of the countryside"*. Opening a new hostel on Dartmoor in August 1935, Mr Raymond Glave Saunders, a former Mayor of Exeter said (as quoted in *The Sunday Telegraph*, 5 February 2006, p18):

"Now that the countryside is being thrown open, the urban population is at last beginning to realise its beauty. What a thousand pities it would be to lose any part of it! The jerry builder, the speculator, the speed-crazed motorist and those numerous councils without any sense of beauty are all trying to rob us of our countryside. But one of the bulwarks against this sort of thing will be the chain of youth hostels throughout England!"

As the Youth Hostel Association recognised, for anyone really to appreciate our countryside, they must first have an understanding of what goes to make up the rural environment. At its essence this is a question of 'knowing our place'.

As far as understanding the rural heritage is concerned, we are very fortunate in that, over the past 50 years, local historians, archaeologists and scientists have pioneered new approaches to studying the countryside. This has led to major advances in our understanding of 'landscape history' – just at the time that the rate of change in the countryside has been speeding up.

Foremost amongst these local historians has been Professor W.G. Hoskins, who was born into a family of Exeter bakers nearly 100 years ago. While still in his 40s, he followed up his magisterial survey of the history of the county in *Devon* (1954) with his groundbreaking *The Making of the English Landscape* (1955).

The impact that this latter book has had over the last 50 years cannot be exaggerated. Although its content is somewhat dated due to the many advances in our understanding that it has inspired, it is still in print. It remains required reading for anyone keen to capture a sense of the time-deep richness and social diversity that give the landscape of this country such a fabulous identity.

Among W.G. Hoskins' many achievements was the breadth of his historical vision. This led him to embrace the 'local sense of place', as well as the lives of people. He also recognised the 'significance of the ordinary' alongside great events and famous people. Thus the traditional farmstead caught his eye, as well as the country house and the parish church. So, too, the lives of farm labourers were of interest to him just as much as those of the rich and famous. Added to this breadth of vision was his astonishing skill to communicate his historical research as exciting discoveries both on the written page and on television and the radio.

To catch a flavour of the breadth of Hoskins' work, just open up his *Devon* at page 99, where he has rediscovered for us the valiant endeavours of the Rev. Edward Girdlestone. In the 1860s this Devon vicar was already standing up for the rights of the common farm labourer years before the first agricultural workers' trade union was set up by Joseph Arch.

And W.G. Hoskins was adamant that we should not just be intent on reading about rural history or deciphering documents in the archives. He knew it was absolutely essential to get your boots muddy by exploring the landscape first hand. Few of us will be able to lay claim to having set foot in every one of Devon's 450-odd historic parishes (as Hoskins did), but we can follow his example and spend a week or even just a weekend exploring one or two rural parishes.

The publication of *The Making of the English Landscape* in 1955 triggered an explosion in our knowledge of the historic landscapes which still surround us today. I will highlight just four areas of recent research that have been particularly fruitful in making new discoveries.

Firstly, there is the value of *fieldwork* – following Hoskins' call to 'get your boots muddy'. Observation on the ground has led to many new discoveries. On Dartmoor, for example, fieldwork by local enthusiasts in the 1960s conclusively demonstrated for the first time that, far from being a natural wilderness area, the open moorland was criss-crossed with extensive prehistoric field systems. Dating back over 3,000 years, these systems are still visibly defined by their 'reaves', or ancient land boundaries, some of which extend for several kilometres running straight across the moors.

The evidence of fieldwork has been supported by major advances in *aerial photography*. This has led to a clearer understanding of the deep antiquity of the landscape that survives through to today. Long-lost settlements and ritual sites dating back to Roman and prehistoric times have been identified as cropmarks or soilmarks on aerial photographs. In Devon, major advances on this front have been made by Frances Griffith working over a period of more than 20 years.

Thirdly, we now have much better knowledge of the *historic buildings* (especially the ordinary vernacular ones) that play such

87

a part in giving different parts of the country their distinctive identities. A key factor here has been English Heritage's comprehensive resurvey of the official lists of buildings of historic interest. Devon has benefited especially from this new survey, carried out to a very high standard, starting in the late 1980s, by some of the leading buildings historians in the country.

Lastly, alongside fieldwork, aerial photography and buildings research, have been the advances made through *archival research* by a growing band of local historians, from university professors to local enthusiasts. 'Local history' is now a respected area for academic study. And the advent of the Heritage Lottery Fund in 1994 has given added impetus to community involvement in the subject. The future potential for local history remains enormous, as a visit to Devon County Council's brand new, lottery-funded Record Office in Exeter will quickly show.

Research techniques such as these are now all being brought together in a process known as historic landscape characterisation. This seeks to give a comprehensive picture of both rural and urban landscapes. But our relationship with landscape does not depend solely on how much we know about it. It also depends on how well connected with it we feel. For rural landscapes can arouse deep emotional responses in us.

This is an area where artists can make such a contribution alongside historians. It is simplistic, but true, to say that we are today creating the heritage of the future. Our decisions on

new development and on choices over land management will shape the landscapes of tomorrow. And artists can play an inspiring part in helping us appreciate the power and purpose of the decision-making process. At the same time they can work as part of this process to mould impressions of change as it happens.

In Devon the contribution of the artist to the process of change has been highlighted by documentary photography, particularly the work of two outstanding photographers – Chris Chapman and James Ravilious. Both these photographers have committed their creative lives to capturing their own local communities and landscapes over a quarter of a century or more.

Chapman has focused on Dartmoor and its surroundings. His poignant photographic essay of the last working days of the wonderfully named Truelove Farm in south-west Devon was followed in 2001 by his painfully shocking images of the impact of foot and mouth on the livestock at Ramscliffe Farm.

Ravilious spent his working life in the little-known lands bounded by the rivers Taw and Torridge in north Devon. His series of books culminated at his death in the images contained in *Down the Deep Lanes*, which is surely set to stand for years at the pinnacle of rural documentary photography.

I have earlier indicated that the writings of W.G. Hoskins are required reading for anyone with a serious interest in landscape history. In my view, engaging with the images of Chapman and Ravilious is also a key factor in helping us connect our factual knowledge to a genuine empathy for the risings and fallings of life in the countryside. Just as Hoskins inspired a new generation of historians, so we can look to new generations of artists being spurred on by the work of these two exceptional photographers.

Hopefully, a reader who has followed my thoughts this far will by now have gathered what "C is for ..." in the title of this chapter. It stands for Change.

Some people will always feel that change is a threat to the conservation of the countryside and to the diurnal course of the world around them. But, as I hope I have demonstrated, change has always been with us and it always will be.

We cannot make the countryside stand still. It is only by the sympathetic and positive management of the forces of change that we can pass on to future generations – both rural and urban dwellers – a countryside that they value and can feel at home in. And when it comes down to it, what we pass on to the coming generation will be the real test of how successful our endeavours to deal with change today have been.

Suggested Further Reading: *Here are ten books, all with a Devon focus, that are recommended for anyone interested in exploring the historic landscapes we live in. All are obtainable through the excellent Devon public library system.*
The Making of the English Landscape, *W.G. Hoskins, Hodder and Stoughton, 1955*
Devon, *W.G. Hoskins, Collins, London, 1954*
Devon's Past: An Aerial View, *Frances Griffith, Devon Books, Exeter, 1988*
Down the Deep Lanes, *Peter Beacham and James Ravilious, Devon Books, Tiverton, 2000*
A Corner of England: North Devon Landscapes and People, *James Ravilious, Devon Books, Tiverton, 1995*
Silence at Ramscliffe, *Chris Chapman and James Crowden, Bardwell Press, Oxford, 2005*
From Wild Goose to Riddon, *Chris Chapman, Halsgrove, Tiverton, 2000*
The Report of the Devon Foot and Mouth Inquiry, *Ian Mercer, Devon County Council, Exeter, 2001*
The Buildings of England: Devon, *Nicholas Pevsner and Bridget Cherry (eds), Penguin Books, London, 1989*
Transactions of the Devonshire Association, *Volume 132 for 2000. This millennial volume contains a series of essays reviewing Devon's past, present and future.*

After his childhood ambitions to become a jockey fell at the first fence, **Simon Timms** *became County Archaeologist for Devon. Landscape history and community learning are among his particular interests. A Fellow of the Society of Antiquaries and a chartered town planner, he was appointed a member of the Board of Trustees of the National Trust in 2005.*

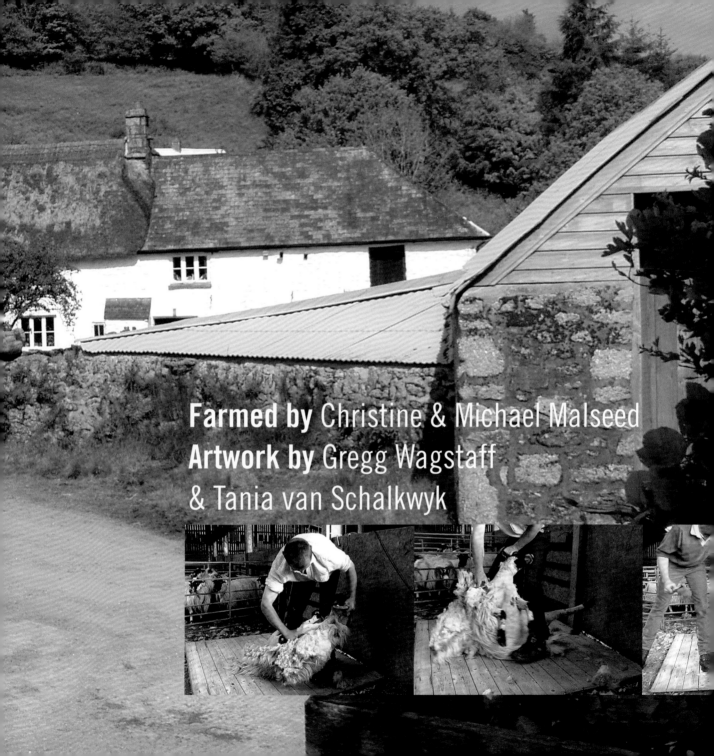

Farmed by Christine & Michael Malseed
Artwork by Gregg Wagstaff
& Tania van Schalkwyk

Shearing Magnolia

Gregg Wagstaff
& Tania van Schalkwyk

There's a garden next door
where a gardener works –
the Land,
cutting and pruning
loving and cherishing
Her –
Crockern
(the land lived, worked and died upon).

He has petal eyes
the colour of his favourite magnolia
                              tree's
inner flower – green veined with
                              crimson
moving to a milk skin as sung of in a
                              1001 nights.

He is in love with his magnolia tree,
calls her Chameleon

as he stands there –
in clothes colour-coordinated to his
                              eyes,
and the garden he takes care of.
Even his voice is
soft with green.

The next day,
when I meet an oak wood
called Wistman, famous in biodiversity
                    circles, for its unique location
– on top of the moors –
I am shown lichen. I touch it and it is as
gentle as the gardener
and similar in hue –
Crockern? Crockern? Crockern?
Are you there?
I'm sure She speaks to him

through the leaves of trees
and the compost in the soil.

The wind carries stories
and pushes me forward

Wet sylvan remembrance
moist with recalled idylls.
'rustic'? 'pastoral'?

Theocritus, Virgil,
Petrarch, Mantuan,
Sannazaro, Tasso and Guarini.
Spenser, Pope and Ambrose Philips.
John Fletcher and Ben Johnson,
          Christopher Marlowe,
Walter Raleigh, Mary Herbert and
                    John Milton –

What *would* you
write about this?
Is this Arcadia?
The land of satyrs,
nymphs, dryads, fauns
and shepherds, who —
— when not seducing one another —
can eulogize
on love, poesy, death —
can satirize
politics, society, critique corruption —

This stills strip is taken from the short video 'Shearing Magnolia', a collaborative work developed by Tania van Schalkwyk and Gregg Wagstaff on Frenchbeer Farm. The video features Tania reading the poem which appears on these pages.

I suppose it's 'As I Like it' really —
I could read a million and more
myths, legends, stories,
fables out of this land —
There is no escape from
Crockern's call
as I tread past trees so green,
you must be able to suck the sap
and never wake up from a tale never told.

the flowers, they're pregnant with
                                    poems
teasing me into pastures of purple
                         prose. Tantalized,
I walk on, and feel like Alice
wandering-wondering about
a land cultivated 'in beauty'.
Or is it 'for beauty'?
Will 'Beauty Save the World'
as Dostoevsky once proclaimed?
Famously? Notoriously?
Naïve? Prophetic?

Crockern is a crucible
and the dew that drops at night from
                    the wings of moths —
chrysalis dreams forming in the drool
                of a sleepy open mouth
is actually the spit of the pot,
bubbling forth its clear bouillon from
                                    deep
inside
out
onto the grass —
that looks so moist
and warm, ready to wrap you in a fur
                    of tropical air —
but feels cold with the frost
of anger biting toes
hungry for more soup. Crockern pours
Herself from winter into summer,
washing us with colours,
so many hues of green, white, orange,
                         pink and
so on and so much and so much, on and
                              on —

late 1960s, and they also have rights on Chagford Commons and a 1,000 acre moorland 'newtake' – the Dartmoor name for the kind of enclosure that the Hawkins have. The Duchy of Cornwall encompasses 70,000 acres of Dartmoor, which is about one-third of the Dartmoor National Park. Although much of the Malseed's farm land belongs to the Duchy, they also rent land

---

pissing fecundity into our
          mouths and eyes,
ears and noses, until all
orifices are full. And yet the hole remains
wounded and open – spilling
a pupae's blood onto the ground.
The search for sustenance continues
boring into the crust of Her body, spirals
through the dark crumbles of earth –
(that we want to package and
genetically modify into little pots
so we can grow small herbs and plants,
control the seeds of Her existence.
And we will never more
be at the mercy
of Her breast
crying for more and more and more)

And still,
Her hand turns the pot's
Spoon silver and gentle
alchemical crepuscule melted and
                              waiting –

Sssht! Its so quiet here!

I can hear so many things.

Can you?

Can you hear Her?

Crockern?

"If you scratch my back,
I'll break yours!"

"Eat Me! Eat Me!"
I think She says –

"Partake of my body
and you will know ever –"

No! No. It's the grockel of sheep
Ewes, Rams and Wether,
Lambs, Hoggety
2 tooth 4 tooth

6 tooth 8 tooth
Broken Mouths –
being sheared.

Are the shuffling sheep
'ecloguing'
amongst themselves about the good old
                    'dog and stick' days
like two shepherds in a pastoral play
discussing today's contentious issues?

Decoupling?

Ponies and Passports?

The high brown fritillary artillery?
– of violets, bracken, little grass and
                              more heat,
just enough (not too much)
nectaring bramble and thistle –
discussed and tended and created

from the National Trust and private landlords. The Malseeds are Mike, Christine and their children Katy, who was 13 when the *Focus on Farmers* project took place; Rosa, who was 11; and John and Richard, both aged 9 at the time. The Malseeds have been at Frenchbeer for 18 years and are first-generation farmers. Christine's father worked in the fashion trade in London,

by Nature, farmers and ecologists on
Common Ground.

And as Vladimir Nabokov once noted:
"It is astounding how little
the ordinary person notices about
butterflies".

If not the fate of pupate,
then what of subsidies and ecological
schemes?

hay meadows, bluebells, cows and deer
woodland
all spread out before us to walk through
with our dogs and picnics and
city-slicker golden-age
dreams —

— COUNTRY LIFE —

a commodity
cultivated by

a subsidized cattle and sheep hill top
farmer turned landscape
preserver.

sylvan heaven
breeding
religious fervour — at the end of an era.
Humans and Nature
Living together in romantic harmony?

— Archaic Arcadia —

the moor looms over head
rough and ready for everything — the
farmers slowly move
away to a more easily cultured and
cultivated land where
the elements do not stunt oak trees,
central heating is only
a field away, and ancient knowledge is
lost —

OR HOW ABOUT THE REPURCUSSIONS
OF FOOT AND MOUTH?

Yeah. "Lets talk about Responsibility."

And —
why do they call the person who does all
the books, sorts out the accounts,
runs the house, rears the children,
plucks turkey feathers, walks the dogs,
counts the sheep, studies a degree in
agriculture, cooks the meals, tends
wounds, works as a professional adviser

to other farm families, apprentices as a
milker on a dairy farm…

The Farmer's Wife?
why not call her
The Farmer?

And with this new legislation —
where are all the dead lambs supposed
to go?

The farmer flung the lamb — dead
into the woodland below us. It looked
plastic
in its rigid state, like those farmhouse
toys I played with as a child, like
the tractor and bright red ear muffles
driven
and worn in a countryside barn,
like a very noisy quad bike
zooming across fields of idyll pastoral
stuff —
unreal?

The magazines I read
never show machines intercepting
where humankind communes with
Nature
— unless it a sexy '70s car with
a tiger on the bonnet and a babe at the
wheel —

95

Mike's father was a vet in north Devon and the couple met at Seale-Hayne Agricultural College. The farm is worked with the help of Jason Thomas, an employee. Christine works part-time on the farm, in addition to three days a week as a farm business advisor for a local enterprise agency, covering north Devon, Torridge and West Devon. The 1,300 acres is spread over four

"*I couldn't have picked a nicer farming family and more beautiful location on the moor. Thank you. I really settled in there and get on great with Mike, Christine and the kids — who make it a joy! I'm already looking for other ways of returning to be there after Focus on Farmers wraps up. The Malseed's genuineness and openness has really made my job an interesting and rewarding one. I hope I can in turn produce something for them, which they will look back on to cherish.*" Gregg Wagstaff, from mid-project evaluation, 29 July 2003

96

Funny, how its softness
inside continued –
warm wet and red
even when –
outside
The lamb was stuck – in an eternal
                                    position –
glued by death like a non-flying
                    non-aerodynamic model
                                    plane.

The fox had incised a
hole into the lamb's side,
accessed an organ-ic(?) feast.
There was no torn flesh,
nor shards of meat –
as expected from a late teenage
            propensity to watching
        midnight werewolf movies –
only a mortician's peep hole
into the original cause of death –
pink lungs spotted black –

"Pneumonia"
said the farmer as he
held his dead livelihood in his hands.

These grim reaper hands
are the same
gynecological hands
that helped give birth to the sheep,
now being shorn by
the same hands
that will drive to the slaughter house

hands —
in sickness and in health
that protect – from blowfly, bramble
                            and barbed wire
hard hands
worked soft by the fleece's grease
to have and to hold
these hands
are leared to the land
to honour and to obey
hefted to Crockern
(She's here)
to love and to cherish
'til death do us part.

**Tania van Schalkwyk
June 2003: Kestor Way,
Chagford, Devon**

Crockern: is the tough spirit of Dartmoor land, often referred to in masculine terms. Here, Crockern takes on a female persona.

Grockel: is the Devon term for crowds of tourist traffic.

locations on north-east Dartmoor, including 200 acres at Whiddon Farm which includes an ancient deer park, and 800 acres around Postbridge encompassing Wistmans Wood, an ancient upland oakwood in the valley of the West Dart River, which is designated a National Nature Reserve for its mosses and lichens. Frenchbeer is a traditional, family-run hill farm with 600 hill

Tania van Schalkwyk

Farm Art

animal hide (skin and away)
slide past fur to moist inside
animal hide
slide past feather and fur
moist inside

beyond pony eyes

further than the grey sludged matter of
turkey's ears

poke through the substance to not find
any meaning
with ruminant's hooves
beating the land
to a tale of ecological scope, not
maudlin but still felt in
lives lived as breath meets the air
merged, with different meanings

slide past the fur and feathers
hear them breathing the land
feeding the hand that feeds –

turkey eyes dark and flat
poignant against the pastel washed out
colour of a peacock palette
rubberized and wrinkled, smoothness
lost to dangling pieces.
run in frenzy. make some noise.
tick tock beat the clocks of their heads.

unlike the peaced up twitch of ponies
soft rolling heads like hay meadows
butterfly lashes and nuzzled shanks
whorl and hoof
smell the skin musked wild
slide past the hide.

beneath the skin of a cow
lies a complex rumination factory –
5 stomachs eat roughage cellulose
grass –
one stomach hosts essential amino acid
creating beasts.
methane burps.

slip past hide and wool
lamb of a tiger deity,
brambled traps weave stolen clouds of
skin,

scrapie jaws open up
to eat the debris
and spit up hard ram horns,
shell shaped and marbled
to walk the land.

these are fields of ragwort wars,
the poppies have long gone and the
hands slide through hide with purpose.
the soil's skin
fleshed out by moles, sings of reality.
the animal and people stories written in
grass, hay and pellets, fly.
and road kill badgers draw a pedestrian
pass-over for the angels of
mercy
as clouds film proceedings without care
for meaning
esoteric obfuscation dissolves in the
solid experience of farming.

a painting of fur feather and hide
whispers of the intricacies of
the flesh
of how hooves and hearts beat, mouths
and hands feed,
the mystery of transubstantiation rises
with each breath in the cold
air
dancing cross country as it slides past
skin.

Tania van Schalkwyk
November 2003: Trim Street, Bath

97

ewes, spring lambs sold in the autumn, 120 suckler cows and spring calves sold at two years. They also have 3,000 turkeys, some of which are free range, reared from June until December, and sold to quality local shops across Devon. The turkeys have gradually increased in number and are now essential to the economic viability of the farm. The farm is heavily committed to

Solstice Eve

White Horse,
Hanging Stone and
Quinton's Man –
spread out under the sun –
melt. Blurred by abundant
beauty, the view from the moor
rises in colour –
fields silaged yellow
sitka spruce green timber
purple molinia grass –

once upon a time,
there lived a farmer
somewhere
near here, at the head of the river Teign
who wrote letters
to himself
so the postman would come and relieve
                              him from the
overwhelming sight of
so much –

it can feel alone here –

even with the noise
of a quad bike and land-rover
chasing cows, calves and bulls
up
for summer grazing –
('til the 1st of September according to
              one ESA contract) –
on the deciduous leaves of a grass
seasoned mauve and palatable now

but Autumn lignified into a hardness
                              sucked
up
from granite ground – beneath.

The volcanoes erupted
a long time ago and
created this land
hued soft by summer light – built
              harsh through elements
mortitioned
in the tips of tors
etched
Wild Rippa Watern
pointing past erosion
Crockern's nipples sliced
erect
in weather that pushes
past human comprehension and stones
                              out of walls.

Tania van Schalkwyk
June 2003: Kestor Way,
Chagford, Devon

The Patchwork Quilt

food and paper, telephone and radio,
                              blue neon
of the fly zapper coagulates with the
yellow hazed straw lampshade
              sheltered energy saving bulbs
and through the window Autumn light
                              flies in past green grass
and stone buildings to illuminate dried
                              moor flowers, bananas, pots
                              and pans,
keys a tweed jacket and homemade
              glass lanterns hanging from
                              wooden beam hooks,
above

a big kitchen table, encased in chairs
              and a former church bench,
                              surrounded by four
children's school paraphernalia, fruit
       bowls of oranges, apples and kiwis,
mail and magazine piles under which

a remote control car speeds faster than
                              the flies buzz, the phone rings
                              and
the radio and TV can talk of the world

scattered amongst

a black hearth and red Aga conjoined
to a dish washer and today's newspaper,
                              cornered

98

environmental management, funded through the Dartmoor ESA (Environmentally Sensitive Area) scheme, with management agreements for land use with agreed environmental objectives negotiated in partnership with bodies such as the Duchy of Cornwall, Dartmoor National Park Authority, English Nature and the Devon Wildlife Trust.

by a floral armchair and countdown
zooming microwave

family photos and children's drawings,
farm related paintings and a
clock
collage the walls and doors

the kitchen's clamour of colour is warm
and seeps
past stone, wood and plaster boundaries
to meet the coming winter

Tania van Schalkwyk
October 2003: Frenchbeer Farm,
Devon & Trim Street, Bath

Mare

Today, the autumn clouds
arrived, prolonged night's cast on the moor,
the shadow that chases
sunlight up and down hills,
dark hooves galloping through,
spread like marmite on a piece of bread —

you can sit along Mariner's Way, meandering above Frenchbeer Farm
when dusk calls the animals to respond noisily before
sleep —

and watch it run across the land, hibernate
the fields' colours, horizons obfuscated.

Tania van Schalkwyk
October 2003: Frenchbeer Farm, Devon & Trim Street, Bath

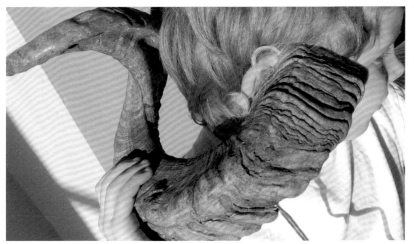

Tania van Shalkwyk created
headphones from rams' horns
and a lounger covered with the
fleece of a Devon Longwool sheep.
Recordings of her poem could be
heard through the headphones.

99

The Malseed Lectures

with Mike Malseed,
recorded and edited by Gregg Wagstaff

On Being a Farmer

Mike: I think I've always wanted to be a farmer, as long as I can remember, and I've always been fascinated by it and done it in my own small way by keeping guinea pigs, getting my first sheep when I was eight years old. From the age of eight I spent all my time or spare time on a local farm in North Devon, and it was the most idyllic lifestyle, looking back on it now. I knew that the sort of farming that was done in lowland Devon in the late sixties and early seventies was doomed really because it wasn't sustainable (we're talking about extensive agriculture) and the only place that was going to be maintained in this country, was where it was going to be supported, and that was in the hills. So it was always a conscious decision to be a hill farmer of some description, with the added bonus of being a hill farmer and farming the most beautiful places in the country, in my opinion. So that's why I wanted to be a farmer, I mean that's why I am one.

Gregg: Your parents weren't farmers then?

Mike: Well my father is a rural vet so going around with him from the age of, well just able to walk really, you've got an insight into this lifestyle. They are not farmers, but they are rural people.

On Dartmoor Breeds

Mike: Dartmoor is unique. You know we've been driving around, talking about all these different hill breeds of sheep and cow, none of them are local breeds really. They are all from Scotland or from Wales or from the North of England. Dartmoor has no indigenous true hill livestock. It has indigenous livestock which are its South Devon cows and Greyface Dartmoor sheep and Whiteface Dartmoor sheep, but they are not what you call true hill breeds and were always just put on the moor in the summer months. Very often the sheep were sent away off the moor, otherwise they get pine, which is cobalt deficiency, and years and years ago they didn't realise why they were pining, they didn't realise that it was cobalt deficiency, but they knew that if they sent them away down to South Devon for the winter, they were fine when they'd come back, and they'd survive the summer. If they didn't do that then they were in trouble. The cattle, the South Devon cows, although this area would have had its own variety of South

Sound artist Gregg Wagstaff worked at Frenchbeer Farm with the Malseed family. As part of that work he conducted a number of interviews with farmer Mike Malseed. Gregg writes: *"When I was travelling with Mike he would often talk passionately about various issues pertinent to farming, in particular to hill farming on Dartmoor. On a couple of occasions, when we had reached our destination, he joked 'and there endeth the lecture.' More often than not the microphone would be switched off. So I asked him whether he would be happy to talk on these subjects for the record. And so, they came to be known as The Malseed Lectures."* The extracts on these pages are from those lectures.

Devon cow that would be a bit more hardy, they were sort of a dual purpose breed for beef and milk, and they were just grazed on the moor in the summer; some of them were let out in the winter to just roam around and back again at night time. In the summer more cattle would come in from all over Devon, but mainly nearer to Dartmoor, to graze the commons and the centre of the moor, where the grazing was let by the old quarterman, who used to rent the grazing from the Duchy and sublet it to other people, and then they'd look after or employ someone to look after the stock over the winter. That's all gone now, and over the last 100 years people have ventured away and seen these true hill breeds that can survive on the high hills in the winter as well, and they've brought them back. So now on Dartmoor, you could see almost every hill breed from the UK represented on Dartmoor, because everyone has their own idea of what is best.

Gregg: What would they be, for example?

Mike: Mainly Scotch Blackface sheep, and all the varieties of Welsh hill sheep, and then there's Swaledales, the Lonks, the Dalesbred, Shetlands, you name it, really.

Gregg: Why is it that Dartmoor doesn't have its own indigenous highland breed?

Mike: I think it is because Dartmoor and Exmoor are relatively small and Bodmin Moor, they are small moorland or hill areas within a sea of lowland, so they are influenced by the lowland farming. It would have been lowland farmers who would have said 'how can we use this moorland to our best advantage' and they'd just adapt their breeds to suit the moor. The Dartmoor Greyface is very similar to the Devon and Cornwall Longwool, it is just an offshoot of that breed. Whiteface Dartmoor has similar roots, it is a similar type of sheep, whereas if you go to Scotland or to the North of England, the whole area is hill area, so they have to have a breed that they can use there. They haven't got the fall back of the lowland just down the road. I think that is why it has developed why it did.

101

On the Hill Stratification System

Gregg: Can we go back and just explain the system of breeding with the hill stock?

Mike: Hill breeds of sheep and cattle are kept because they are adapted for those areas, they are hardy, the cattle have got shaggy coats and are very good foragers. They don't grow particularly fast because the quality of the forage isn't good enough, so they grow slowly and they come to sexual maturity later than lowland breeds. They are superbly adapted for their environment, and they have good mothering skills, because they have to when having a calf or a lamb in a harsh environment; they've got to be good at it and they are. That's one of the benefits that lowland farmers get from hill breeds, especially sheep, because there is this long established system whereby hill sheep when they get to a certain age, about six years old, and they've had the best of their life and they're in decline almost, they are taken off, usually to an upland area, a less harsh environment, and then they are crossed with a long wool breed and they produce lambs which go down to the lowland farms for breeding ewes, and they inherit this good mothering ability from the hill breed, and they get some other attributes from the sire, which is generally size and prolificacy (because the hill breeds are not that prolific – you only want one lamb really). In the lowland you want at least two lambs from your ewe, and in the hill area, most people want just one lamb. You cross them and then you get this cross-bred lamb, and also they exhibit this hybrid vigour, so the offspring is better than both of the parents. These

go onto the lowland and have in the past formed a huge proportion of the lowland breeding flock. The same is true of a lesser extent with the cattle.

Gregg: So do you sell your sheep on, down onto the lowlands for fattening up?

Mike: Yes. We finish a few but most of them will go either for breeding, because we sell these cross-bred lambs for breeding, others go for further fattening to be killed. Ones we don't keep for our own replacements are all finished in the lowlands.

Gregg: Finishing being the term for fattening up?

Mike: Fattening up is not a term we use any more because fat is not a good thing in people's perception, so you are not, you are putting flesh on them.

Gregg: But finishing could mean (*makes noise of slitting throat*).

Mike: Yes.

On Art

Mike: There is an artist near here who is a sculptor and works in granite, and just up there is a rock which has been split in two and it looks almost like a fruit, it is not a fruit, but it looks like there is something living inside. You know.

Gregg: Do you remember his name?

Mike: Peter Randall Page I think he's called.

Gregg: And that is sited there, is it?

Mike: Yes, there are some all the way down the valley, you come across them, almost in the middle of nowhere. You know what I was saying about Damien Hirst and so on, but you look at this and you instinctively know it is art.

Gregg: You like it?

102

Mike: You can see that there is incredible skill gone into doing it. Incredible, and it is very effective. You've taken something inanimate and it looks…

Gregg: Organic in some sense.

Mike: Yes, really clever. It is not very far up there, you want to go and have a look?

Gregg: Yeah! (*They arrive*). What a wonderful spot.

Mike: Don't you think that's clever?

Gregg: Who is the artist again?

Mike: Peter Randall Page. He lives here locally.

Gregg: So this is a big lump of local granite is it?

Mike: Yes.

Gregg: Kind of a sphere which has been sliced in half, polished, and then this is inset, metal? In the shape of a maze.

Curator Simon Ryder commissioned an audio/visual table containing four stations to view the videos and DVDs, and to listen to various sound recordings and interviews with the farmers and their families. Around the table, and placed across the exhibition space, are 20 folding chairs upholstered with the same hunting print fabric as hangs in the Hawkins family dining-room on Exmoor.

Mike: Some of his other ones, they are sculpted inside, they are contoured instead of this flat surface. It looks like it was something that was living, or is living.

Gregg: Like a nut or a shell or something.

Mike: Yeah, or an animal.

Gregg: I thought that it was going to be polished rather than another material inset in it.

Mike: I've never really looked at that, but it is, isn't it. It is lead or something.

Gregg: It could be lead. So you appreciate the time and craftsmanship that has gone into that artwork?

Mike: Yes, well it is a local material so it is in the right context and I think it is quite effective. You walk through the woods here and you just stumble across it, and he's got several similar pieces throughout the area.

Gregg: So if we compare this to Damien Hirst's piece where we've got the mother and calf cut in half, what did you think to that? Did you actually see that?

Mike: Just the calf. I think that piece of work, Damien Hirst, I can't… to me it's just a dead calf cut in half, that's all. I think people might be interested in it, or it could be shocking for some people because they don't come across that sort of thing, but being a farmer, you come across things like that, so if he's trying to say something it is kind of lost on me.

Gregg: Maybe there is an educational aspect to it don't you think?

Mike: No. What are you talking about? Anatomy or something?

Gregg: Mmmm.

Mike: There are better cross-sections of cows, I'm sure, to be learning anatomy from. I'm sure it's because I don't appreciate these things, I think

103

some of these modern artists are having a laugh really, and it's like the emperor with no clothes, people don't dare say he ain't got no clothes on. These art critics and everyone say 'it's marvellous', pay a lot of money for it, and then they are laughing all the way to the bank, but that's just my narrow prejudiced opinion! (*He laughs.*) But this – slaps the Peter Randall Page – is money well spent. It will be there forever, really.

Gregg: It is a bit difficult to judge, therefore, something like poetry and sound, which in itself isn't an object, it's like a performed or temporal event, isn't it? If we're kind of qualifying art as an object of craftsmanship…

Mike: Yeah, but to a layman, if it is a poem or a recording, there is something inside you that it hits a chord with, even if you might not understand it, you think you know what they are trying to say even if it hasn't got to the uninitiated like me.

Gregg: I'm glad you brought us up to see these.

Mike: This is only the second time I've ever been here.

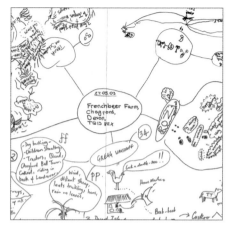

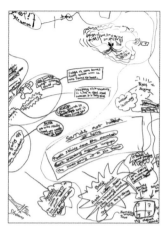

This image belongs to a sound mapping exercise by Katy, Rosa, Richard, Tania and Gregg. Paper was spread out on the Frenchbeer kitchen table and each participant chose a different colour marker. The time and place was written in the centre, along with their names and ages, before they proceeded to work outwards, drawing or notating in any fashion a sequence of sounds heard from waking to sleeping. Other categories of sounds were also introduced, for example, 'favourite sounds' and 'sounds you don't hear at Frenchbeer'.

105

There
Phil Smith

Before

There is an imagined space I am preparing to walk into, thinking about footwear, about the wind and the cold. About the place and how to feel it. And then there is this phantom space where I keep my theoretical maps and imaginary photo albums, a state of mind. On top of all that is the way the land is thought before I get there, after I get there, after I go. Hanging longer than the leaves. History, I suppose. Waiting to be shaken.

I am in my attic office when the phone rings. Nancy from AHA: would I go and do the Runnage Farm Walk created by Beth Hamer and Kirsty Waterworth for *Focus on Farmers*? Well, yes, I would very much like to. Thank you. And so I was laying out some phantom spaces before setting off.

In my head I would be entering an ancient industrial area. A site of illusions about bleakness. The tourism industry seems to like unspoiled territory. Is there something colonial, rapacious about that? The hearty rambler casting a dark, old shadow.

I hadn't set off yet and already these layers were interweaving their grids. Lustful at just the thought of the walk. Becoming a web.

And then there is Runnage farmer Phil Coaker's voice on the telephone. I feel slightly ashamed. There is a workedness in his rush and matter-of-fact friendliness. I cannot quite rearrange the contradictions to speak to him sensibly. We talk out of time with each other.

I know I will be coming into a contested space. I know enough to know that animals need to be fenced and gated in and that fences and gates gate and fence out. That this will be a place of work and necessary exclusions and signless meanings, of the frequent birth and death of sentient organisms and that these farms are hyperpolitical, the sites of national controversies: BSE, foot and mouth, hunting, retail monopolies and subsidy.

More especially for me these are places where the roles of animals and humans are ambiguous. Animals that are de-wilded and yet not domesticated, tamed and ordered and the objects of an industry. As alien and valuable as molten metal. The farmers too: guardians and stewards of the land, nurturing for slaughters. I eat meat, I expect to see death. I wish more death was visible. I remember my daughter at two years old watching the light in the eye of a cartoon Stegosaurus fading and asking me to play it back, checking what she had recognised for the first time. I see no humiliation in death, only in pain and oppression. So I would be a hypocrite to even find the expected ambiguities difficult. Farmers are jugglers too, of the market and of the rhythms and chemistries of nature. My prejudices (greed and naivety that had them stitched up by the supermarkets), sympathy (for anyone who feels the soil beneath their feet moving to the vibration of economics), dislike for nationalism, shock at a right wing sticker illustrated with a cottage…

And my distant family roots in farming. I have a photo but little memory of chasing chickens. Adolescent wanderings in the Warwickshire countryside. Hanging over the bridge at Cubbington watching a pike hunt, a hilltop and a girlfriend, an expedition on bikes ended at rectangular pools full of years of rain and newts. I wouldn't find those playgrounds of friendship and surprise and eroticism again.

And there are deeper ambiguities. In my head is an ancient Britain with lowlands covered in forest. Not dark fairytale forests, but deer-thinned park-like woodlands. On the sparse heights like Dartmoor there are human communities, farms more or less fortified, on treeless, not impossible soil. 'Bleakness' that is a human thing, rather than sublime. Settlement, yes, and trajectories too: in recent centuries the postman's way, the track to take animals to market, death walk, spirit path, a route for tramping labourers and for children leaving for the town, then ramblers, lanes for agricultural salesmen in Ford Populars, the wholesaler's agent and vets. Ridiculously, I imagine this as historical. Green lanes and hollow roads, conservatism and the dull, cyclical thud of the annual rhythm.

Going

I caught the (late) 8am X9 from Paris Street in Exeter. The doors of the first coach were broken. The driver raced to make up time, while things changed on the other side of the condensation. Met Jennie in Fore Street, Okehampton and we drove off in her black boy-racer. She said in her email, "*I am not a boy-racer though*". She drives like fluid, setting off with a guess. We arrive after no wrong turns, spotting the sharp right-hand fork after Postbridge and the Clapper Bridge which I remember from holiday stops for coffee after the 3am start from Cov'. I step out waiting for 'nippy' farm dogs. I've been swayed by vehicles for two hours now. The dogs are calm, quiet and watchful. Christine Coaker comes to the door and after a quick chat in the kitchen with her and Phil I set off.

Driving across the moor, I'd clocked the nomadic architecture: trig points and isolated gateposts; accidental menhirs. Astro-archaeology started near here: at Drewsteignton with William Chapple, eighteenth century Powderham Castle accountant. Long the practice of crazies apparently, now mainstream archaeology eats humble star-gazy pie. But I can't quite buy the certainty of geomancers, though I like their plethora of vectors and the poetry of small designs standing for bigger things. They are part of my sticky web: half safety net, half trap.

To say thank you I give Christine and Phil a set of the Crab Walking maps made with Tony Weaver. A little of the rented land in my head.

Outside the farmhouse door I can't pretend to know what I'm doing. Like at the start of writing a play. I have to learn it all over again. Why have I been asked to write this? I am just another juggler baled out by micro-gravity. What I know of other disrupted, eccentric walkers slows me, swirled in memories. I can pretend to myself there is a discipline I follow, and there is: a dictionary of spaces, a fluency in signage. And narratives from one walk picked up in another. These are parts of the mental map of my own mythogeography: a skein of nonsense and science, history and lies, altered states and Fortean analogies. Strung around me, I have to be a pilot of my autobiography.

My Dad flew a Vampire, cross-country, over the moor. From RAF Merrifield to St Eval. I fly pedestrian, civilian, close to the ground. But I will walk with my Dad's trail above me.

Map

Closing the farmhouse door behind me the rush of detail bewilders me. All the clutter of organisation, camping barn and signs for visitors, cricket bat, hose, the detritus of entertainment (faded red light bulbs and benches) beside kennel, spade and the practical ridges in the concrete. On this scored working space, the discarded wash basins and accidental theatre behind the camping barn give me something to hang all these sights around: an intensely practical play of decay. Useful bits of broken roof are becoming a wall, bust ornaments block holes, where useless but harmless broken things are left, marking time. The farm is layered with timescales, the protective coat of an ecology that is susceptible and vulnerable to longer rhythms, comings and goings, and the rush of things to do and guests like me. I get lost and read "we shan't go that way". The bloody book is trying to take off – two white limbs flapping in the sharp wind. I struggle with it like an incompetent shearer.

I had read Beth and Kirsty's map in Exeter before coming to Runnage Farm. In the street outside our house the wind had been stirring the blue balloons announcing the birth of our neighbours' son. I kept looking up, a prehistoric pathway in the brain making me jump. In the corner of another old eye is my imaginary Runnage Farm, made from Phil Coaker's voice and a comic flick through the book: "beware of the bull" – I'm already 'walking' it, the low level paranoia in my toolkit triggered.

"Steady!"

In one of the photos I mis-read the gaps between trees as huge white icicles.

I imagine completing the walk. The broken teeth of the granite barn at the walk's end look to be a welcome. Filling in a wish-list I once wrote "aged 90 between the teeth of a white whale" for "how would you like to die?"

Will the final hanging still be there? After walking in the footprints of princes?

I like the elusiveness of the pictures in the book. They remind me of the generality of the original illustrations to John Bunyan's Pilgrim's Progress and the sweeping arrows of Guy Debord's psychogeographic maps of Paris.

I should have been prepared for all that

early granularity in the farmyard: the book is ingrained with seeds, punched with an address, seared with a brand. Burnt "*C*". The cover grimed by earlier users.

Two weeks before the walk, I had sat by the 747's window on a flight back from China. The straightened veins of irrigation systems and the fencing of installations gave way to green clumps around rivers, then dry hills swept up like grey sand against a wall. The light faded and there was darkness. Clouds crowded in below and, as if we were flying over some terrible war, orange pads of light glowed under the sickpuffy clouds. Somewhere North of Ekaterinberg a frightening point of yellow seared the white below like the brand on the book cover. I will walk with that beneath me.

The rack of bikes in the lambing sheds. A crow crackles. A barn door taps boomingly.

I had been in Shanghai to give some talks on *Macbeth* for the British Council. One of my themes was the sacred body of the monarch; the royal frame as the conduit between the divine and the world, balancing conflicting forces and transforming tension into a motor. It's why Shakespeare lasts. He doesn't choose between Protestant and Catholic, commerce and aristocracy, text and picture, classical and popular, but he mediates; his most tragic, evil, royal characters are the most individual and most commercial in emotions, their modernity doomed to happen.

Nowadays, the bodies we look to most to mediate for us between ourselves and 'all',

totality, nature, are those of animals. Different, diseased, grown to eat, experimented upon, groomed, wild, filmed, anomalous, escaped, Aslan, pets, species stamped out by our environmental footprints, Great White Shark off Padstow… hmm. Moo. Baaa.

In the wind the brand "*C*" flails out in scorch. The photographs edge like smoke. Identity: a set of tugged veils, clouded, seen under water. I cannot grasp them, cannot imagine the route.

"*Walk straight on*" – how is that possible with this map?

Pit

I've come the wrong way, but don't know yet and I busy myself in the detail, putting off the moment of disorientation. Stuck at the cow sheds and silage pit. Words and pictures don't add up. I'm working the wrong sense. The hollow sockets of the cracked tyres stare upwards, like an empty-eyed 'fakir' in my great-uncle Bill 's 1934 copy of Ripley's *Omnibus Believe It Or Not!* In a few minutes I'll be sinking up to my shins in the camping field. Trying to read the subtext of green surfaces. The first sinking moment, you don't know how deep it goes. That's how I feel about the kicking map. That I'm walking on the green skin of a brown ocean. That I don't know the rules. Don't understand the instructions. Back at primary school, trying to read by pictures. And that doesn't help either. I hear Phil Coaker's whistle to the dogs. I hear the whistles in the map, I know I'm beckoned, but not to what. Can't work it out. It only last a few moments, but it shakes me up. Just right. Upsets what's left of my complacency.

"... we shan't go that way."

And I walk in the tradition of Stephen Graham, Stephen Murray and Charles Hurst – eccentric walkers of the early twentieth-century who broke from the healthy rambling and race walking that had been the orthodox pedestrianism for half a century. Each disrupted by their own 'thing' – Graham a love of 'tramping' (unplanned wandering), Murray by fascination for walking in the abstract and the historical, and Hurst obsessed with oaks, boxes of wrapped acorns in his pocket. They all slowed down. They all gave up on destinations. Graham loved to negotiate his passage across farms – having drawn a straight line on his map he attempted to follow it. Hurst lodged in farmhouses and recruited farmers to the cause of the oak. All in revolt against an escapist rural walking that had somehow managed to re-programme itself like the city's timetables and production targets: for 'health' and 'improvement'. So I'm wary when I walk. Of hidden agendas. The Surrealists, wandering into the middle of France, fell out.

In the yard down from the farmhouse the gates into the pen had wormholed me to a similar ordering, enclosure and sorting elsewhere: on the side of a heavily secured yard on an industrial estate in Taunton. I had been walking to an edge of town multiplex to see George Romero's fourth film in his Zombie trilogy: 'Land of the Dead'. But both here and in Taunton I'm wormholed by the metal portal grilles to his 'Day Of The Dead' where the zombies are coraled, fed, sorted for experiment by the military. The subject becomes the object. The "pen" is the cutting edge of animal and human. A prison. A passage. A communication. An ordering. A differentiating.

Later, after the freedom and panic on the moor, I return to another "pen", policed by two adult and one young pony. I skirt them. Horses and ponies are in the field on the other side. "Beware of the bull". No bull. Just the Houyhnhnms, those authoritarian horses encountered by Gulliver on his travels, looking mildly and affronted. I'm anthropomorphising them, using my "pen" to order them, to rearrange things according to my fears. My nervousness about difference. Wanting to simultaneously collapse it and police it. I know what the Houyhnhnms do – apparently so noble despite their lack of alphabet, we can forgive them their extermination of Yahoos. We like horses. We like to reserve a general right to atrocity against others. Just in case. The "pen" is perfect for this moment, caught between relief at getting in and apprehension at getting out: knowing that every moral response – respect, care, stewardly management, conservation – will mean nothing without alphabet. Without the branded "C". A human sheep, I am. For a moment someone else's cursor on the map. Not looking into eyes. Sliding down the hedgerow like a geometrical exercise, listening inside for the sound of trouble.

The gate on the right opens up to a big field, sheep at the top curved and arched like the moors beyond. Their black faces, commas. Even though I cannot see its boundaries I feel free to be spooked here. I enjoy the sudden zooming of the view. As I walk down the bowl of the hill, all around seems gently curved. The ground bulges warmly beneath my greened boots. I stop. I don't feel alone in the big field. But ghosted in a comforting way. A dangling rucksack strap taps my leg. Inside something creaks. Above, a jet. I think of Dad and the Vampire. It all feels calmingly geometrical again; the layer of sound above, the Venn Diagram hills, the hieroglyphic sheep.

Writing this across a screen, letters like the eggs of flies, patches of paragraph like the damp warning of maggots on a sheep's coat. Of flesh eaters. But I didn't think of that in the field. I felt the cosy shape, the car running along the bottom hedge, the whole thing conspiring with me. I'm not surprised, but pleased when the field yields a playground against the hard bushes, breeze blocks softened by lichen, serpentine dead gorse stems and settings of concrete weathered long enough to look considered. Chance and piled. Ready for reverse-archaeology – ruins from which a monument to the future might be constructed.

The road beyond the gate at the bottom of the big field is refreshingly wet and it shines and twists. The green verge is luxuriously humped. I'm self-possessed again – starting to begin the process I'm ending here: re-ordering, mythologising. Trying to place "*pen*" in the order of things: a path blocked with dark firs, a crash of farm machinery rusting beside a puddle like an abandoned Caro sculpture.

The day after the walk it starts to make sense to me – this is perilous and, in a way, the point: that as the enduring present of the experience is prised away from what it was, the lies of the land begin to settle, the territory, so neutral and 'there' then, is disrupted, frozen in parts, and begins to slide across the experience in swathes. I am a cursor on a screen, clicking on 'moments', aware of the running plane across which I spread.

Local

I have tried to understand how I got so lost so early on, so near to the start, so worried then that I would mess the whole thing up and waste the day. AHA had sent me a dvd of essays already written for this book. I found this by Lucy Lippard:

"If topographies change at a glacial rate, the cultural landscape is constantly transforming and so are we, its inhabitants, its transformers. A cultural map may be all centre and no margins, also a definition of the truly local, where each centre within a centre is connected by paths to other centres."
I never escaped my own imagination on the walk, but just about everything else. The

margins were stripped from my shrinking centre. The whirl of other centres was hallucinatory. This might be a walk chosen by hypnotists. They push you hard up against anxieties: about where your place is, what your way is, who you are here. To curl the mind around with those connecting paths. Later in her essay Lucy Lippard writes:

"Perhaps art about agriculture or nature itself will not be fully effective until it goes under-ground, until it is integrated into and almost disappears into local culture and nature itself."

This walk begins your disappearance. It sends you off. Like the best artists of place, Kirsty Waterworth and Beth Hamer work space for its trajectories. Not a lone path bounded by instructions, but a matrix tripped and tickled into digressions and, then, new tangles by strands of connecting suggestions.

After a clumsy crossing of the stream, flapping the book, I ripped off into the gorse. Following the stream as if it were the farm's boundary. I'd mis-read *"you are now outside the farm's boundaries"* to mean that. I headed out across the moor. Yet where would the next *"pen"* come? Once again, the map was pulled from beneath my complacency. My ease in the bleakness – the tall poles of Sousson's Woods and the yellow motorway driven through it – is disrupted by the local I don't know. I slip between things.

At one level it is the farmer's eye for detail – a wet patch on a sheep's coat. Watchful for something. Idea bugging out. And at another level this is part of a national park, a farm of the Duchy of Cornwall. I felt these two layers: the close, local knowledge of work and flesh, and the idea of all this space as nationally and socially significant. I was sliding between them. But in the granite barn I would see them reach out for each other. That's how I imagined it. I was headed for that, unknowingly. Later Jennie described Phil Coaker's practical generosity to the artists, helping them hang the piece in the granite barn. Sending the farm-hand to fetch a ladder, considering alternatives to baler twine.

Lost
Phil Coaker had appeared at the gate into the camping field and I was relieved that I could confirm with him I was going the right way. I like a map that sends you up the wrong path and then says *"we shan't go that way"*. But actually it had shaken me. I'm glad of Phil, a working landmark I can re-navigate from. The map is only doing its job. I've stopped being the 'expert' and started being buffeted, super-sensitive, worried that I'm not going to do this walk, but lose myself uselessly, unproductively on a farm. That's when I sink up to my shins. Pushing off from a bed of water. Fortunately, the camping field firms up. Breeze block campfires and black hunched lumps of gone fire. Order. Stop.

Inside a *"secluded"* and soggy bit an unreal caravan sort of hovers. Getting to firmer ground I understand the haze around the cream camper. There's a grove across the stream and I feel the first dread of my walk: the pleasurable rush of low level panic, the titillating precursor to feeling free to do, sensing suddenly the scope of possible. I'm somewhere I can recognise: where tourism and paganism meet.

"What I'm trying to articulate – and inevitably stumbling to do so – is that walking acts as a kind of enchantment, a way of opening up breaches in the whole spectacular mindset that so dominates everything. Lyotard's notion of the landscape as a series of shocks and surprises would fit here. Walking allows you to ENCOUNTER the new constantly. It breaks the landscape up – any landscape up into fragments – and thus, in my view, produces lines of imaginative flight, daydreams and reverie. The paradox is that these lines of flight are not evasions – they do not flee something. Rather, they produce the city anew, and are thus a flight into something. Above all, they are PRODUCTIVE. ALL POWER TO THE IMAGINATION AND TO COMMUNITY OF REVERIE." (Carl Lavery from a post to Sue Thomas' blogsite at http://writing.typepad .com/ digital_life/2005/09/walking.html (11.11.05))

A community of dreaming on the hoof. The farm just as re-producible as the city. *"Something with no purpose – no means, no end, no purpose"*: Phil Coaker on blow flies. But waste I like. Playing in the derelict future is at war with jobs to be done. Is it? For this is the waste of art. Waste that can be spread. Excessive rather than lazy. So what will be the exact quality of the contradiction between us?

Just before I sat down with Beth and Kirsty's book I had been on the web. I'd ordered a cheap VHS copy of 'Dark Skies', a paranoid TV series mixing recent American history with ol' alien greys. Returning to the Amazon website the next day they threw up a *"recommended purchase"*: a 'Dark Skies Map' for astronomers, charting darkness, deep over the moor. When I get across the brook I walk in darkness during daylight.

I'm drawn to the eyes in the book. The dog's eye. The eyes of the sheep. The eyes of a cow that seems to swivel its body around its look. A farm is a place of alien consciousnesses. About the assumptions that I had before walking the book I now have to set in motion these shifting views and looks, big unknowns that I find hard to face. They are like whole beaches suddenly lifted and breaking: the inexplicable, unthinkable thinkings of cows and sheep and dogs.

I hope the chandelier is still there.

113

Hung

Beyond the caravan and the 'grove' the green carpet rolls out smooth, finished and finessed and I just seem to bowl up it. I can see the hole in the wall I'm heading for. After all the uncertainty underfoot and the liberating dread, the farm becomes comfortingly geometrical for a while, a smooth grid I can walk slowly and feel fast and very green and light. The surface like a map. Making me a character, a part of an alphabet, a figure – half theatrical and half statistical. Partly adept and partly tourist and enjoying the friction.

But Beth and Kirsty are going to shake all that up again.

Over the fallen wall is the Wallabrook and I must *"cross by the stepping stones"*. But the water level is high and they're submerged. I pace up and down looking for an easier crossing. There is none. I place my foot four or five times on possible leverages, but each time step away, the stones shifting under my weight. I'm jumping a shifty boundary. I lose all sense of sliding across the map. I'm sinking through it again.

On the other side of the brook I set off into open moor. Christine said that one walker had gone for hours with the book. She ended up at The Warren House Inn on the B3212. Like me she must have taken the stream for the boundary of the farm, but not veered left hard enough and was lost to the gravity of the farm. I nearly followed her… but felt things fragment and liquifact. Just as I was understanding my pleasure in the brook's environment, the moss green like miniature tumps, rocks modelling canyons, a natural geomancy of something bigger. Then: I'm not doing it right. I'm missing the point. I re-jump the brook and bend hard to the left, up and across what seems like a very old path marked with trees, back to the walled

boundary, shockhead lightbulb trees, and then the pen and all that.

Down the snaky road to the sign for Runnage Farm, I turn in at the gate. There's a broken door up against the right-hand stone wall. In fact, all around the farm there are broken gates and unhinged doors, discarded or doubling for walls. A sort of reverse Narnia, these are closed off escapes. The serious commitment to farming. A lifetime.

Coming up the concrete ridges of the farm lane I get no echoes of the generations. They're there, but for their own reasons. Not performing for me. Instead, I feel a reverse version of the moment in Fiona Templeton's New York walk-performance *You-The City* (that I've only read about) when the walker/audience realises that they have become the actor, that they are doing now what earlier they had assumed was the work of an actor and now realise was a walker just like them. But I'm not the actor, the path is, and all the associations of Vampire, Shanghai and Romero thin and fade. When we drove in I saw the lane for its function alone. Now it's that assumption played back: that practical doesn't perform. But it does. Full of gestures, curved like an arm. The lane is the mediating body. Concrete. Real lane. The intense pattern of stacked fence posts. All detail. As if an actor left her script on the stage for the audience to read. With all her notes.

Under a line of beech, I turn into the last field. The bottom wall is a parade of broken gates and large stones. The two dogs appear upon it like that horror film trick when the camera pans away and back and they're supernaturally, silently, suddenly there; all eyes.

The air in the granite barn is colder than outside. A sack remnant hangs like a regimental banner in a cathedral. There's a perfume of secret belief. The thick quarried slaps of granite, forbidding palms, castigate, wall up, Old Ones – looking, for all the world, like a straightened-out stone circle or an astro-archaeological row shuffled up, shoulder to shoulder, closing ranks against divisive details. Flames. Orange and green. A sudden fall of wax. The chandelier is a crown of many crowns, a crown of cutting and riveted things, a crown of ploughs, a weighed thing, a lowered thing, a harrowing crown. Suspended on butcher's hook and builder's pulley. The mediated and mediating body reappears, rustily ceremonial and under pressure. The animals cleared out. The absent landlord and king in waiting. The magical and the social. Hung by farmer, farmhand and artists. A bitter perfume in the gloom. A hard future. A smoke ghost. It's here. Unfilled.

It is a privilege to snuff out the flames and cough on the wick smoke. Now I can, unlike the farmers, walk away.

Beth Hamer and Kirsty Waterworth's Runnage Farm Walk is both treasure and dragon, looping back on its walker. The busy textures, the dread, the lostness, line, "pen", curves, snake, lane and stone grin – they chuck you about and rearrange what you think about difficult things. The walk swallows itself

productively, wastefully. Putting these things smartly, industriously together. Farming the means. I hope I'm not the last.

Phil Smith *is a writer, theatre-maker and explorer of the already discovered, a member of Wrights & Sites and one of the co-authors of the Mis-Guides to Exeter and Anywhere. His thoughts on walking are available at www.rhizomes.net/ issue7/issue7.htm & http://reconstruction.ws/031/TOC.htm*

Reading list *for anyone interested in reading more about exploratory walking:*
The Gentle Art of Tramping, *Stephen Graham, Ernest Benn, London, 1929*
The London Adventure Or The Art of Wandering, *Arthur Machen, Martin Secker, London, 1924*
A Mis-Guide To Anywhere, *Wrights & Sites, Exeter, 2006*
Walkscapes, *Francesco Careri, Editorial Gustavo Gili, Barcelona, 2002*
Wanderlust, A History of Walking, *Rebecca Solnit, Verso, London, 2001*

with Kirsty Waterworth & Beth Hamer

Recorded and edited by Jennie Hayes

The beginning of autumn, a cold sunny day. Phil and Ricky are busy hiring out 16 mountain bikes; Christine sorts the paperwork and helmets. I park behind the tractor. Kirsty and Beth are examining what looks like a chandelier lying on the ground. It is a chandelier constructed from old farm machinery. They take it to the barn, with a large length of rope, while I chat to Christine. A friendly farm dog comes to be petted. Kirsty and Beth return and we go into the kitchen, having asked Christine if its ok, to have a cup of tea and a chat.

Jennie: What were your expectations for the project, why did you get involved?

Kirsty: Being able to work down here and do a commission locally based was really important for me. I felt I knew Dartmoor, I thought I knew about farms but knew that I didn't really and I loved the idea of spending 28 days in someone else's home; that opportunity to live a life as somebody else does, to experience a different way of life.

When I first came I was keen to observe and do as they do and so was helping as much as I could and I wasn't actually producing anything myself – I don't think I got the video camera out for the first four days at all... To start with they got to know me, as 'not me at work' me, although part of the process of working was that observing and experiencing, but I think once I started actually getting the camera out, and the more we've become independent and we've started to work... really quite intensely collaboratively, we've been moving off much more on our own and pottering around the farm doing our thing...

Beth: ... I guess it's very odd having two people following you around and having to explain everything and having to answer questions that don't particularly interest you probably; you've maybe got more important things going on than people saying, 'oh so how many times do you go to market?' stuff that is so mundane and so everyday, and for us really interesting... I guess it took a lot of energy for them to really be explaining the whole time...

J: What about your original expectations, Beth?

B: I was really interested in doing some work on Dartmoor, that was my initial attraction to the project; and working collaboratively; and working with different media – I haven't used film before, so it was good to have that opportunity. And get involved in the farming community and understanding that and, like Kirsty said, we come from Devon, we've lived around farms. It's been to some extent part of our lives but actually we don't know that much at all....

K: We do now!

B: We had quite a good footing to start with, that confidence really, so it wasn't so daunting, it was ok to go for it and completely submerge ourselves in it and be very open to learning more...

K: In some ways I'm not sure if that's a bit of a handicap that we both know Dartmoor and we've been around farms and maybe came to it with slightly preconceived ideas of what it was going to be. I have to say that the Coakers (Phil and Christine Coaker, farming at Runnage Farm) are totally different to what I expected a farming family to be...

B: But I don't think our expectations have been allowed to follow through...

K: What do you mean?

B: My expectations of what this project might have been, or how I wanted it to be is so very different now after the reality of spending so much time with people... it's really changed...

K: I think we both had quite romantic notions about what a residency on a farm might be and the relationships with the people...

J: In what way is it different?

K: Time-wise, it's a funny thing, if it had been two weeks, part of that romantic preconception of what it was going to be like would have been fulfilled. But the longer its gone on...

B: But that's exciting as well, because we're no longer relying on Phil to answer our questions or give us a reason for being here. Our reason to be here is to make our work and that's a lot clearer now and we're really fired up about that and that's what we're going to be doing.

K: The minute we started doing our own work it changed the whole thing...

B: And we have gained independence from the farm in a way, which I think they probably find quite hard, because not knowing really what we're doing and although we're explaining it's...

K: It's still an unknown quantity for them, isn't it...

B: ... and they are quite hard concepts to grasp and sometimes we're a bit unsure...

J: What have you learned about farmers and farming?

K: It's hard because we both feel that Phil is different from the farmers around here...

B: But even a Devon hill farmer, you know, baler twine around the waist, straw out the mouth, really broad accent, that kind of thing. Phil is completely not that at all, although he's lived here his entire life, he could so easily fit into that stereotype or that idea that you have of a farmer.

K: I like to watch him interact with other people actually… obviously, he's in a very dominant position, he can show us farming however he wants us to see farming. It's not until you see him in other scenarios that we can build up a bigger picture… I think the point of the residency is to see farming warts and all, but I'm not sure how much we have seen it warts and all and how much we have seen it in the way they have chosen to show it to us.

J: You think in some ways it might have been presented to you? Even although you're obviously really involved here…

B: But then again I don't think we are really, really, involved. We could be a lot more involved and the fact that it's two days, three days, four days; it takes you a day to get into being here, get used to the whole thing, forget about whatever you've come from. You've got a couple of days to get into it, then you're on to the next thing. When I first heard about the residency I imagined it to be in a solid four-week block, which really appealed to me, great, you can really get absorbed into the project, it will become your life for a month, and that really attracted me, then it wasn't like that…

K: … I thought one of the things that would interest me most would be the human aspect of the farm. But having to be so intimately involved with the human aspects actually made me shy away from dealing with it because I don't feel it would necessarily be appropriate. The times I feel most inspired to investigate that are the times when I'm feeling negative about it, which obviously isn't what I want to portray and that's not what it's about for me or the project… It almost feels that you're doing a piece of work about your friend, but they're not your friends, I'd like to think I'll maintain a relationship after this and if I'm driving by I'll always stop in for a cup of tea but I don't feel I can make work about them.

B: Yes, it's too close.

J: It's interesting that the intimacy of the working relationships actually provides a block…

B: There's also a responsibility – if it was a complete stranger you could just push it, but it's almost like you owe them gratitude…

K: You have a bond with them…

B: And you respect that, so it's not worth going there.

J: Does that mean that you wouldn't want to produce something that they might find hurtful? How does that responsibility sit in terms of your work?

B: That's definitely an issue and it's frustrating – there is so much that you could do, when you're angry or upset, that's a great time to produce it, but you have to hold it back, and say, no, just deal with it, just let it go… there's far more positive things that we can portray from our experience here.

J: I wanted to ask you how important you think it was to have some kind of understanding about the social, political and economic context of agriculture today…

K: It's important in terms of the relationship

with the farmer and the farming family, it would be disrespectful if you sat here at the table without even having a clue what goes on. You are invading someone else's home so to go into it not knowing anything about it, to me personally, would have seemed wrong. I don't know that much but I tried to know as much as I could...

J: Kirsty, you said something about already having a bit of understanding and participating in the daily working of the farm... you... try and participate, get immersed, understand the context before you make work?

B: The passionate element has definitely come up for me, I've really found that... in conversations about contemporary farming issues that I have strong feelings about, but I'm also really willing to discuss them, having those discussions with the farmers in their kitchen drinking their tea, have become quite entertaining.

J: Have either of you shifted in your views through having those discussions?

B: Yes, it's been eye-opening. It's always good to hear the other side and hear it first hand. Phil is great, he really wants us to learn, issues such as foot and mouth, he really wants us to know the insides and the outsides of that, he's got time and energy to talk about it. Quite a few discussions we've had... we've ended up realising that we've both been coming from the same space...

K: I'm not sure how much that is true, though. When you and Phil sit there at the end of the conversation and say, *"but yes, so we're both saying the same things essentially"* and actually, they're not. You can both believe you are, but listening to it and not participating myself, I don't think you actually are.

J: Have any of the family been involved in your work, in an active sense?

K: Christine and Phil have both used the minidisk. Christine set it up to record the sheep shearing, which I was really pleased about because we both missed shearing, so at least we can hear it, or hear them singing to Shania Twain anyway, whilst shearing; and Phil took it out to do his own talk through the fields. We were talking about doing a sound recording walk across his fields and Phil decided to do his version, which was really interesting and he thoroughly enjoyed doing and he's talking about doing another one. So, having initially gone *"we're not going to use that minidisk"* they've both used it. I've done nothing with Richard (Phil and Christine's son) other than during silage he became a camera director for a while and told me *"shoot this, shoot this, film this"*. But he didn't actually play with the camera. But you've worked with him...

119

B: Yes, I've done quite a bit, but very much at the beginning, before our work started to take off, I did quite a lot of drawing with him and chatting about the different ideas of making work. He had to make a vegetable animal for Widecombe Fair so we were discussing things like that and explaining to him what we're doing. I was really keen to get involved in the family element, I thought that kids as part of the farm was really interesting... I'm glad he is here and at least we've had some child contact... different things are pointed out to you, different stories are told. It's good.

J: What do you think actually happens when you as artists work very closely in this environment with people who aren't artists? What happens that might affect you or your work or your process of working? What makes you work differently or think differently?

K: Certainly for me it's made me have to validate myself more, justify myself, my work, my way, which has been useful for myself and hopefully for them.

B: We've been far more interested in farming than they have in art, which I guess was inevitable, but I was kind of waiting for them to ask or to say, 'so what is going on?'. Their lives are very busy, they have to go and feed their animals, you can't get distracted, you have to get on with your job, whereas I guess we can, to an extent, if we don't do it now, we can do it in an hour. You can't do that when you're working with animals. So I guess that's cut down time or interest that hasn't allowed for questions or learning.

K: I don't think I necessarily expected them to want to investigate us particularly much.

B: I did.

K: Beth was able to come in here and have totally different points of view and be more than happy to voice them. I'm much more of a chameleon, come in, adapt, change. I'm not

reluctant to talk about it, but they haven't asked and I'm not going to push it. I'm not going to throw art at them in any way, shape or form... I never expected them to show an interest...

B: ... and I guess that has also related to us not showing our work to them all the time... it's the evening, half past eight, Phil maybe comes in and he's completely exhausted, he's been out since 7 o'clock in the morning... and all he wants to do is sit in front of the TV and say nothing to anybody and fall asleep. We can't invade that... he needs that time and we're in his living-room and its great that he feels relaxed to do that...

K: So we're not going to prod him and stick a video on and say... *"look, look"*...

B: So we have to organise time... a special arranged time.

B: Also our work isn't...

K: ... it's not quite so tangible... we're recording sound but the sound isn't the work, we're shooting video but it's not going to be a single piece of video, we're collecting objects but it's not going to make an object, it's very difficult...

J: Do you think that the project will do what it aims to do? You used the term *"elucidate and educate"* (from the Aune Head Arts brief to artists).

K: I worry that there will be an expectation that 'elucidating and education' are easily gained and I don't think anyone looking at our work will immediately be educated and elucidated by it, but I like to think that Aune Head Arts are open to the idea that it might take a few viewings and a little bit of reading about our work to fully appreciate it. I'm hoping that it doesn't have to be immediately evident.

B: The origins of our work are very much about contemporary farming issues…

K: Our work is steeped in it but it's not immediately visible.

B: But I like that, it's more intriguing, it's not obvious when you come here. It's something you have to work at, that's been part of the experience and that's come through in our work. As a viewer, I really enjoy work where I have to interact and I have to think why? What's it about? How?

J: What if Phil and Christine found the work difficult and couldn't relate to it but you felt it worked?

K: I'd definitely like them to come away with a sense of pride, not necessarily actually in the work, but in what it does; it's their farm and ultimately their ways that we have been investigating… I mean I don't think they have to be able to understand it and relate to it and 'get' it. I don't think there's a problem with them going, "Well, why have you done it this way?". That's all right. But I would like them to be able to say to their friends, "Yeah, look, this is Runnage". It comes down to that responsibility thing. I owe it to them for them to be able to walk into that space and go, "I don't get it, but yeah".

B: I think that will happen, we have talked a lot about the work.

K: I think they'll be surprised to realise how much they know of the work already. They have listened to our rubbish conversations all the time and taken part in them to an extent. The fact that both of them took the minidisk out, after having heard us talk about doing the farm walk; "All right, I'll do that then". We're hoping to include Phil's stuff in it, watching the pride he got from listening to the piece he'd done, so if we can incorporate that into the bigger piece…

B: It's having some ownership or inclusion in the work. There's got to be some… they've got to be included. It's not like just coming here and taking away what we've got, it's about sharing that.

After the interview, Kirsty and Beth go out to the disused barn to discuss the hanging of the chandelier. Phil comes to see what's happening. They spend some time discussing the weight of the piece and the best way to hang it. Phil sends Ricky off on the quad bike to fetch a ladder to hang the chandelier. Phil stands above the piece lying on the ground, and bends over to have a closer look. He says, "I'm impressed".

Farmed by
Christine & Phil Coaker
Artwork by
Kirsty Waterworth & Beth Hamer

The Coaker's Runnage – one of the 'ancient tenements' of Dartmoor – sits alongside the Walla Brook, a headstream of the River Dart (and eastern boundary of the Forest at this point). Like Frenchbeer, Runnage is a tenancy of the Duke of Cornwall and, unlike Frenchbeer, is almost entirely enclosed fields. Philip Coaker's father and grandfather were the Duchy's agisters for

The two artists resident at Runnage Farm, Kirsty Waterworth and Beth Hamer, had very different approaches to artmaking. At the time Kirsty was working mainly in video and Beth was very interested in collecting found materials and creating objects with them. In putting them together on the same farm, AHA hoped that a fusion of their interests and styles might take place.

Both were keen to collaborate and they worked at finding a common creative language. Over time the influences of each crept into the developing work – Kirsty began to expand the physical qualities of her work and Beth experimented with video. The finished works are an example of a highly successful collaboration.

Cycle #1 Kirsty Waterworth & Beth Hamer

When silage-making was in full-swing Kirsty explored ideas of incorporating the colour and text of the lush grass into an artwork. She grew a 'screen' of grass onto which she projected this video loop of a lamb leaping. Over time the image of the video began to imprint itself onto the living grass.

the east 'quarter' of the Forest. An agister supervised, leased and could sub-let grazing on the Forest before it was a common and in a sense was an agent for the Duchy. Philip grazes on the Forest now under licence from his landlord who, with all owners of common land, is entitled to 'the surplus' after the 'commoners are satisfied', and can make it available to his tenants.

This traditional moorland farm of about 220 acres has a rich past, dating back to 1304–05, when it was first recorded as an ancient tenement of the Forest of Dartmoor. The Coaker family has lived and worked here since 1843. Like all high moorland farms in the area, Runnage concentrates on livestock production, in particular cattle and sheep. The Coakers sell their own

Situated Frustration

Kirsty Waterworth & Beth Hamer

beef and lamb, and run camping barns and cycle hire businesses alongside their traditional farming. The Coakers also own 30 traditional Dartmoor ponies, which are out on the open moor. So, the four homesteads of the four families that are the subject of this book have much in common and yet great variety as far as their context is concerned. Greenwell is lowest but most

The neon number is Runnage Farm's personal Defra (Department of Environment Food & Rural Affairs) identity number. The nine granite stones were collected along the Walla Brook – Runnage Farm was sited where it is because of the importance of a source of water to farming. The first (and largest) rough granite stone was taken from the spring at the head of the brook; the last (and smallest) smooth pebble was found much further down the brook's course. The seven stones between them (of various shapes and sizes) were found along the line of the brook as it descends through the farm's land from the higher, open moor, to the lower, enclosed fields.

Situated Frustration in location during the exhibition at Buckand Abbey.

exposed. The other three are higher, within 350ft of each other but all slightly more sheltered. Greenwell is almost certainly the oldest, Warren Farm by far the youngest. Runnage and Frenchbeer have the same landlord but a quite different land-base. While the Dartmoor folk have all – in modern parlance – diversified and thus have other strings to their bows, all four pitch

Farm Walks

Kirsty Waterworth
& Beth Hamer

Phil Smith takes Farm Walk

A series of self-guided walks was developed on Runnage Farm. Kirsty and Beth created a Farm Walk with directions outlined in a hand–made book and, as part of the project, Aune Head Arts lent each farm family a minidisk player, encouraging them to use it to contribute to the process of capturing life on each farm. In interview with Jennie Hayes, Kirsty Waterworth says:

"Christine and Phil have both used the minidisk. Christine set it up to record the sheep shearing, which I was really pleased about because we both missed shearing, so at least we can hear it, or hear them singing to Shania Twain anyway, whilst shearing; and Phil took it out to do his own talk through the fields. We were talking about doing a sound recording walk across his fields and Phil decided to do his version, which was really interesting and he thoroughly enjoyed doing it and he's talking about doing another one."

AN AUDIO JOURNEY WITH PHIL COAKER
(RUNNAGE FARM 2003)
[Sound of Phil whistling.]
    "Come on dogs!… hello Max… good dog… hello mate… come on dogs… you alright? Come on then!" [Whistles.] "Good dogs…"
    [Sound of footsteps, gate opening and closing, quad bike starts up.]

"Come on dogs... steady! Steady! Wait... come on then..." [Dogs bark.]

Just rounding these up. In there we've got about 70 sheep, these are what we call a commercial sheep, they are cross-bred ones, a meat-producing sheep really. These are the sheep that we cross with the Texel ram which is a very well-shaped, well-muscled, well-fleshed ram and that gives us fat lambs that we send to market or send to the abattoir. *[To the dog]* *"Steady... Max! Good boy... stay down!"*

Also we've got some black-faced lambs which are sired by a Suffolk ram. Suffolk's a black-headed, black-legged sheep with white body, white wool, very solid well-muscled sheep again. That's another sire with a ram suitable for producing fat lambs...

We grow a field of kale each year... [*whistles*]... just got one sheep breaking... dogs have got it back. *[To the dog]* *"Steady... Max!"*

We also grow stubble turnips for the cattle – across the valley I can see that field. We graze those from about 10th October onwards when the open grass runs out. The cattle strip-graze the stubble turnips and are supplementary fed the silage, until about the beginning of December

when they are brought in and housed in a couple of yards, back at the farm. Thats all undercover housing that gets them out the weather, they are dry and warm and they'll stay there for about four, four and a half months I suppose, got to get through certainly until the 20th April, maybe the end of April, it's a very long winter. We have to grow all our own silage to feed them in the meantime, that's all harvested in the summer. We've had a very good year this year, lots of grass. Probably got about 560/600 tonnes of silage, about 500 round bales of silage, about 150 round bales of hay and we still do some conventional small bales of hay the old-fashioned way, the hard work way. We like those to feed them to the sheep when they're lambing and we feed them to the baby cows, they like nice soft hay, it's just better than the silage, really.

So we've got to the gate now where the kale is growing, it's been quite a good year for kale but it's also been quite a good year for weed. We've got one or two undesirables peeping up between the leaves of kale. We've got lamb's tongue and another called red shank, these will die down over the winter period and just leave the kale and that's what the sheep will graze.

You are the farm first gat

129

If we move on a bit further… the purpose of re-seeding the land is to make the grass grow better, and of course if we give the grassland a break from growing grass for maybe one or two years, by growing crops of kale, it's a deep rooted plant, it brings the fertility up… and also when we graze that kale with the animals, you place the animals on very thickly because it's an abundance of crop and it needs a lot of stock to eat it and they leave all their muck on the land and that helps to improve the fertility again. Whilst we use artificial fertilisers, man-made chemical fertilisers, to enhance the growth, we also rely heavily on the animals. With 200 cattle in the winter, there's a lot of free daily fertiliser, so that can give us a problem with spreading back on the land. If we've got wet conditions, and it's difficult to get the tractors and spreaders out, we have to store for a week, maybe two and then we spread it as fast as we can as there is a lot more on the way! It keeps everything clean and tidy, we like to keep the yards clean as we can in the winter, makes the job seem a bit better if everything is in order.

Walking back up to the road, in the field we've got a lot of clover coming through, which is a good thing, sheep love clover. We've got lots of grass… rye grass, timothy, different things… and both red and white clover. Red clover very often grows wild, to give it a good start it's nice to have a little bit poking through. Sheep grazing quite well. Lot of grass here.

Sounds like people are starting to get up, I can hear the dogs barking, cattle shouting in the farm next door – I expect that guy's out doing his

morning rounds as well.

[Sound of gate opening and closing.]

We're going to cross the road, take the bike down, run the fields on the higher side of the road, we have a big run of land there, about 250 sheep in there… have a good look at them and see what's going on.

[Sound of quad bike and then whistling. To the dogs] "Keep off! Steady… bring them in nice and close… Meg, go back, go back!" Sheep are all coughing well, to be expected being chased around early in the morning, I suppose. *[Whistling.]* That's it. *[Sound of walking.]*

One of the things we're looking for here is what we call fly strike, when the blow flies lay their eggs on the sheep's wool, horrible things. Those eggs hatch into maggots and the maggots start to live from the skin and the flesh, actually feed from the skin and get right underneath the wool and, left unchecked, that can eat a lamb alive, horrible. Flies with no purpose, no means, no end, no purpose. It's something that probably costs us over £1,000, maybe £1,500 a year in preventative treatment and corrective treatment. When we do get a problem there's chemicals we can use that we spray into the wool, that helps repel the flies, but the period of protection is quite short, only about six weeks, maybe eight weeks at the most, then we start running into problems again. The fly risk is from May right through until the end of September, maybe into October. As an individual that's costing me, and if you put that together with a few losses that occur and then work it out on a national scale for all the sheep

131

farmers, it's a huge problem for the industry. It's probably the thing that the sheep farmers dread most. It's the thing that keeps us on our toes, it's the one thing we have to study in the sheep all the time, make sure they are clean and no wet patches. If we've got a wet patch on the sheep but otherwise it's dry on the rest of its fleece then it usually means it's got fly strike and got maggots that have hatched out and started to live, so we have to catch that and treat it. There's one I had to treat yesterday, I can see that one, but the rest look ok. But in summer weather, hot, dry, humid conditions, you don't miss a day on this; if you do miss a day then there is usually a price to pay. It's very much a job that you can't put off. Ideally need to check all stock first thing in the morning, one reason is that a night is a long time, something can go wrong during the night. But the other thing is it's nice to see stock before it gets too hot, because in the heat of the day all you'll see is a load of animals lying in the shade, you can't tell, they're not grazing, not doing anything, just glad to be in the shade and out of the sun. In the mornings we can have a good look because they're usually up for grazing as it's not too hot yet.

132

[To the dog] "Good dog, steady, lie down, leave it..."

We've had a good look at those, we've got further to go, we've got more cattle to see.

[Sound of quad bike.]

[To the dog] "Hey hey hey! That's it, stay, Meg, stay, hup!" We don't want Meg to come with us, she'll stay on the bike, we can walk down.

[To the cow] "Morning girl, alright!" I can walk in amongst the cattle, they won't take a lot of notice of me, whereas if the dogs come they'll disturb them and I won't really see what I want to see. One of the problems we get in cow is mastitis, once again that's caused by our little friend the fly, it affects the glands, the teats, and we get a mastitis infection build up in the cow, that stops the cow sucking, then we have a horrible rancid milky type stuff that we have to remove from the cow, left in it almost turns into a poison. In extreme cases it might severely affect the cow but normally it's just a mild infection, but it's still something we can do without. Just looking for that. These calves are about nine/ten months old, these need to be weaned, cows are looking nice. [Cows calling] "Alright?" One, two, three, four... twenty-three, there's one there, twenty-four, that's it...

Just looking back, the dogs are sat bolt upright on the bike, one on the back carrier, one on the seat, watching just in case I call for them. If I whistle they'll be straight over and the cattle will go everywhere, so we won't do that.

Right, we're going to go back, we're going to ride around, just some more on the opposite side, bit of a boggy bit here, so rather than walk through, ride around

it. It's back to the bike. The great thing about the bike being a bike and not being a horse, it hasn't

The end point of the Farm Walk was the 'discovery' of a lit chandelier made out of found farm objects. Here farmer Phil Coaker works with Kirsty and Beth on suitable methods for hanging it in an ancient barn.

run off, it's still exactly where I left it. I suppose you could say if it had been a horse I wouldn't have had to get off it. Not really winning that argument am I?

[Quad bike starts up.]

[To the dog] "*Stay!*" I'll just walk around these as well... *[To the cows]* "*Good girls...*" They are all pretty quiet, this lot this morning. You can probably hear them walking around but they're not really calling very much. Pretty content.

[Whistles and dogs barking. Sound of the quad bike.]

Now I'm going to get in and have a bit of breakfast. There's still stock left to see, I'll do that after breakfast. Then I think we'll be sorting sheep out today, a bit of foot-trimming and weaning some of those lambs, I expect. I'll just go and see if the calves have been fed.

135

Artworks

Copies of several of the artworks represented in the pages of this book are available for purchase in digital form from Aune Head Arts. By purchasing this book you are entitled to a discount of 30% per item. You can complete and return the form on the dust jacket along with a cheque made payable to 'Aune Head Arts' or visit www.auneheadarts.org.uk and follow the link to 'shop'. When ordering online, use the promotional code FOF0708 to receive your discount.

GREENWELL

Farm Film Tony Hill
(VIDEO) AN INTIMATE PORTRAIT OF LIFE ON GREENWELL FARM

Greenwell Barn Hill/Standen
(VIDEO) A TOUR OF THE BARN WITH FARMER ARNOLD COLE

Farming Greenwell Hannah Standen
In two parts: A Farming Year, Hill Farming in 2003
(AUDIO) 2CD SET WITH BOOKLET

The Greenwell Series Hannah Standen
(B&W PHOTOGRAPHS) SERIES OF 12

WARREN

Rights and 3. Brow, trey 4 Tessa Bunney
(DEER SLOT) A FOUND OBJECT

Growing up with Horses Tessa Bunney
(A3 BOOKWORK)

Photographs Tessa Bunney
(8 SINGLE IMAGES, 2 MULTIPLES)

Photographs Louise Cottey
(12 COLOUR IMAGES, CARD PORTFOLIO, RIBBON)

Wire Fence Weavings Louise Cottey
(WOVEN FLEECE, WIRE, FOUND OBJECTS)

FRENCHBEER

Shearing Magnolia & Lifelines Wagstaff/van Schalkwyk (VIDEO AND TEXT, ALSO ON FRENCHBEER DVD)

Farm Art Tania van Schalkwyk
(RAMS' HORNS HEADPHONES, SHEEP SKIN, CD PLAYER)

Index

140

Acknowledgements & Picture Credits

When Aune Head Arts agreed to take on the publication of this book, after a passing conversation in our front room, we didn't begin to realise the enormity of what we were about to undertake (undoubtedly a good thing). Four years on, the book has come to fruition – but not without the support and goodwill of a large number of people to whom we owe our heartfelt thanks.

To all the farming families – without the generous invitation into your homes and working lives, the project would not have been possible. Arnold, Bridget, Neil and Mathew Cole, at Greenwell Farm, Meavy; Phil, Christine and Richard Coaker, at Runnage Farm, Postbridge; Mike, Christine, Katy, Rosa, John and Richard Malseed and Jason Thomas, at Frenchbeer Farm, Chagford; Andrew, Trudy, Richard, Giles, Hannah and Rebecca Hawkins, at Warren Farm, Simonsbath, Exmoor, Somerset.

To all the artists who approached the work with a spirit of adventure and empathy. We are indebted to you and the creative approach each of you took. Tessa Bunney, Louise Cottey, Beth Hamer, Tony Hill, Hannah Standen, Tania van Schalkwyk, Gregg Wagstaff and Kirsty Waterworth.

A special thank you is due to Chris Fogg and Clare Fisher of Beaford Arts, who were so intrigued by the project concept that they asked to be involved. Their interest enabled the project to involve Warren Farm on Exmoor through additional funding and a lot of hard work on the part of Beaford Arts.

141

To the essayists who wrote contributions for this publication. Anthony Gibson, Lucy Lippard, Ian Mercer, Phil Smith and Simon Timms – all of you took a leap of faith with us at a time when we didn't know for sure that the book would be published. Your thoughtful and insightful reflections have provided a context for the work that encourages us all to 'look again'.

To our investors in the project and the book. Arts Council England South West, the Esmée Fairbairn Foundation, the Dartmoor National Park Authority, the Dartmoor Sustainable Development Fund, the Dartmoor Trust, the Department for Environment, Food and Rural Affairs, Littoral, Teignbridge District Council and West Devon Borough Council, thank you for making this possible. Very special thanks are due to Aune Head Arts' Dartmoor Angel, Kate Ashbrook, who believed it was important to share the wealth of information and ideas from the project with a wider audience.

Separate thanks are also due to John Weir, Head of Communications at Dartmoor National Park, as it was his original enthusiasm for the project which helped us persuade Peter Joyce (then newly in post as the Officer heading up the Dartmoor Sustainable Development Fund) that an arts project could support the goals of the fund through the creation of artworks which examined the cultural, social and economic significance of hill farming on Dartmoor. Our thanks to the Members of the DSDF Panel for their support of the original project and exhibitions and of this book, which ensures that a much larger public will learn about the significance of contemporary hill farming and consider ways in which they can help it to be sustained.

Thanks are also due to AHA's Board of Directors at that time, who agreed it was a project we should undertake: Susannah Lash, Willem Montagne and Joanna Radford, as well as Secretary Jackie Parsons and Advisor Gillian Taylor.

To those who all had a role in making the original *Focus on Farmers* project such a success: Bridget Arnold for being the first to say 'yes' as a host farm and making it easier to convince the others; Garry Hayman, Manager of the Bellever Youth Hostel, for always making us feel at home; Andy and Gabriel at Brimpts Farm for their interest and for the bountiful food served during the mid-project meetings; the Dartmoor National Park Members for spreading the word in the farming community; the Globe Inn, Chagford, for giving us their upstairs room for a meeting; Nell Harrison, who hired heavy equipment and kept us fed during the installation of the exhibition at Buckland Abbey; Rah Rivers, Project Manager, who kept things on track throughout; Rob Steemson, Head Ranger Dartmoor National Park, for suggesting AHA contact the Malseeds as a host farm; the Throwleigh Centre for Young People for their super facility, where we held our final two-day meeting with the artists; Bridget Wren for the fantastic meals she prepared for us at Throwleigh. Thank you all.

AHA is equally indebted to those who enabled the FoF artworks to be exhibited across Devon: Martin Fitton, Chairman of the Association of National Park Authorities; Clare Fisher and Bill Granger at Beaford Arts; Michael Coxson, Hannah Jones and Sally Whitfield at Buckland Abbey; Mike Malseed, Chairman of Chagford Show; Mike Nendick and Karenza Townsend at Dartmoor National Park; Leyland Branfield, then Chairman of the Devon NFU; Christine Jowett at Exeter Phoenix; Rose Gregory at Exmoor National Park; Jennie Wilkinson at Griffiths Yard Shop/Café/Gallery; Maurie Webber at the Museum of Dartmoor Life. Further thanks are due to all those Village Hall chairmen and committees who worked with Beaford Arts to open their halls for the exhibitions, hosted cream teas and made our rural exhibitions such a positive experience for everyone involved.

142